D1614544

LLOYD GEORGE
WAS MY FATHER

LLOYD GEORGE WAS MY FATHER

**UNIVERSITY OF GLAMORGAN
LEARNING RESOURCES CENTRE**

Pontypridd, Mid Glamorgan, CF37 1DL
Telephone: Pontypridd (0443) 480480

Books are to be returned on or before the last date below

First Impression - April 1985

ISBN 0 86383 112 5

© Lady Olwen Carey Evans and Mary Garner

Printed by J. D. Lewis & Sons Ltd., Gomer Press, Llandysul, Dyfed

CONTENTS

INTRODUCTION

Lady Olwen Carey Evans was almost into her nineties when the idea of writing her autobiography was first proposed to her. She had been giving a television interview, recalling as she so often does those unexpected sidelights of her life with Father at Number 10 Downing Street. It all sounded so much fun that someone suggested she ought to write a book about it.

The thing that strikes you most when you talk to her is that life has, on the whole, been great fun. She has an enormous sense of humour, probably inherited from her mother, and she is extremely good company.

When I first met her, it was to write a piece about her for my newspaper, to mark her 90th birthday. Any preconceived ideas I might have had about her quickly disappeared, for there she was, soon chuckling with pleasure over the memories which came back to her so readily. She has an extraordinary memory, and can recall in great detail the many events of her long and interesting life.

Lady Olwen was born on 3 April 1892, the middle child of David and Margaret Lloyd George. If she inherited her mother's sense of humour, she certainly also inherited her father's determination, and her stubborn independence has often been the despair of her family. She is also extremely outspoken, a fact that her father noticed very early on, with the result that he tended to try to keep things from her, for with her acute perception and outspokenness she sometimes caused him great embarrassment.

This was not intentional, for to her David Lloyd George was a hero and a genius—someone who could never really do anything wrong. Even his infidelities, of which she became aware as a young child, were excusable, a necessary outlet for a great man. Suggestions later in life that she had lost all regard for her father caused her much distress, because this simply was not true.

She also inherited from her father his passionate love of Wales and all things Welsh. Being Welsh is one of the most important things in her life. During her childhood in London, her later life there, and her many years abroad, she never forgot the language of her ancestors. She speaks Welsh as a matter of course to her many Welsh friends and neighbours. She delights in her life in North Wales, and she fiercely defends Wales and the Welsh if ever anyone makes an out-of-place remark in her presence. Unlike her brother Gwilym, who joined the Conservatives, and her sister, Megan, who became a Labour MP, Olwen has clung tenaciously to her father's old Liberalism, and is still an active worker for the cause, although she never had any ambitions to enter politics herself.

Looking back over her life, one is tempted to suggest that perhaps of all the Lloyd George family she was the lucky one. The public gaze which caused so many problems for her two brothers, Richard and Gwilym, and her sister, Megan, largely escaped her. She was allowed to lead a relatively normal family life and grow up in her own way. She married happily, and found a sense of deep personal fulfilment in her own family of two sons and two daughters.

Throughout her life she has always been ready to help others, and many organisations in addition to the Liberal Party have benefited from this. The Royal National Lifeboat Institution has always been close to her heart, a reflection of the many years she has spent overlooking the sea at Criccieth. There she has been able to grow old gracefully among her own people, enjoying life and taking an active part in everything which is going on. Until last year, when a broken hip caused some alteration in her life style, she was to be seen driving about in her little car, doing her shopping and visiting her friends. For many years she used to call personally at Criccieth Post Office every week to collect her pension. 'I always said, "Thank you, Father," when I collected it,' she told me on more than one occasion. 'I've never forgotten that it was Father who first introduced the old-age pension.'

Mary Garner.

Chapter I

1892-5

FIRST MEMORIES OF FATHER

When I think of my father, I remember more than anything else the feeling of excitement every time he came home. We always knew when he was there; there was a kind of electricity running through the house. You felt something was about to happen. When he arrived unexpectedly, everything would suddenly become alive.

Life revolved around Tada. He was very good with us children, never too tired or too busy to play with us or tell us stories. But when he was working we had to be very careful that we didn't make a noise or get in his way. You never knew when the balloon would go up!

When I was born in April 1892, Tada had already been in the House of Commons for over a year but continued to live in a house next to my grandparents, overlooking the sea at Criccieth—a spot I have always considered to be one of the most beautiful in North Wales. When Tada wasn't at the House of Commons, he used to travel each day to his office at Porthmadog, five miles away, where he was still a practising solicitor. Later, when we moved to London, he opened a branch of the firm there.

My earliest memories of Tada are of his coming home from the office at 5 p.m. for tea. He used to come by train on the Cambrian Coast Line, which ran along the coast right on the edge of the sea below our house. We knew when his train was due and used to listen for the whistle from the engine as it passed Black Rock Sands and came level with our house. I can still hear that whistle today.

We had usually finished our tea by the time Tada arrived. A tray would be set for him and put on the dining-room table. Everything was set out most beautifully and looked lovely.

One day stands out in my memory because it was the first time I remember my father being really cross with me. He had been given half a dozen plover's eggs—a great delicacy in those days. Mother and we children—there were three of us then—had one each for our tea. The other two were kept for Tada. I remember seeing them on the tray in the dining-room.

When Tada came in he usually had his tea straight away but this time he called to my mother: 'Come on, let's go and see how your father and mother are today.' They went next door to see my grandparents, leaving me in the dining-room. I looked at the tray on the table and saw the two plover's eggs, one in the egg cup and the other on the plate beside it. I thought to myself: I had one of those for tea and it was very good; I'd like another. I ate it. I had just picked up the second one when I heard footsteps in the hall, so I pushed it into my mouth whole. Tada saw me. 'Hello,' he said, 'what have you got in your mouth?' He took me on his knee and said: 'Spit it out.' He could see the debris of the eggs on the tray. I spat out the egg. He put me across his knee and smacked me soundly.

That was my first contretemps with my father. I was in disgrace for the rest of the day and was made to stand in the corner behind the table. As I stood there I fell fast asleep and the maid put me to bed.

When I woke up next morning, I was full of beans again. The maid asked me, 'What did your father do?' and I said, 'He whipped me very, very hard', and then I remember dancing round the room. So I don't think he really punished me very severely that time. But he'd had to go without his plover's eggs, which I think he'd been looking forward to.

There was another occasion when I was a little older which I remember with great clarity. My father went to Rome during the time of the Irish Troubles and saw the Pope. The Pope gave him some sweets; they were nougat and I can still taste them. He gave Tada two packets, one to bring home for us children, and the other for John Redmond who was leader of the Irish Party at that time. John Redmond had four children and the Pope thought they would like some sweets too. Tada gave us the sweets when he got home, and handed John Redmond's sweets to Mother for safekeeping. She put them into the cupboard where she always kept sweets. I liked the nougat very much—so much that, when nobody was looking I went to the cupboard, took the other packet out and ate it all!

I don't remember Father punishing me that time, but I do remember his comment afterwards: 'That was why the Irish question was never settled!'

Tada never came back from any of his journeys without presents for us. He usually gave us boxes of fruit rather than sweets, which he didn't think were very good for us. I think he often used to buy the fruit at Victoria Station on his way home. We were given sixpence a week pocket money but we never had many sweets.

We were all high-spirited children, but we knew we had to behave, especially when Tada was at home. I was the middle one of the family—at that time there were only four of us: Richard, Mair, myself and Gwilym. Richard was often very naughty and always laid the blame on me. I thought this was unfair as I have always hated injustice, and always will.

Mother had a birch rod, but she only had to make a gesture towards it and Richard, who had just learnt to speak some English, would acclaim: 'Oh I say! Oh I say!' That was too much for Mother. She just had to laugh and any idea of beating was forgotten.

Dick was three years older than me and always very mischievous. I was often the butt for his pranks. Once I turned on him and gave him a resounding smack on the face. I don't think he tormented me quite as much after that. We were always very good friends; I used to like playing with the two boys. In fact, at that time I played with them more than with Mair, who was eighteen months older, but as we grew up she and I became very good friends and her death when she was only seventeen was a terrible blow.

We were very close as a family. Looking back I think my father could be very selfish, although he was also kind and generous in many ways. In my eyes he was always right, nobody could say anything against him and I would fight like a Kilkenny cat to stand up for him. He used to say, 'If you are doing anything, do it well.' Although he was such a great talker, he was also a very good listener.

He had a special name for me. I was the only fair one of the family—I had blue eyes and was rather pale. Tada used to call me *Llwyd* (which is Welsh for 'grey' or 'pale') or *Llwydyn*, the diminutive. If he called me Olwen, I knew I was in trouble. I can hear his voice now thundering, 'OLWEN . . .' He never bore any malice or sulked afterwards and when we upset him it was soon all over and we were back to normal again.

When I was naughty, which was quite often, I think, I used to escape from the house and dash round next door to my grandfather. He always knew I had been naughty when I rushed in. I used to stay with him until Mother came looking for me. I had many a slap as a child but I don't think they did me any harm. On the contrary, I think they were very good for me.

The house where I was born and in which we lived at Criccieth belonged to my grandfather, Richard Owen. He was a farmer, and my mother was his only child. The stone farmhouse where he lived for many years and where Mother was born was known as Mynydd Ednyfed. It was on the top of the hill, overlooking the sea, and from it you could see the

The pair of houses which my grandfather, Richard Owen, built in Porthmadog Road, Criccieth. I was born in the house on the right, known then as Brynawelon.

whole of Cardigan Bay. The house is still there and the land around it which my grandfather farmed is now a golf course.

My grandfather owned about 100 acres of land. He worked hard, the farm prospered and he was very highly thought of in the area. I was very fond of my grandparents, largely, perhaps, because they used to make a great fuss of me. When I was small I had a weak throat, and after my parents moved to London I used to spend long periods at Criccieth with my grandparents.

The chapel played an important part in my grandparents' life. They were Methodists and as my father was a Baptist they did not give him much encouragement when he first became friendly with my mother. They met on an outing to Bardsey Island in 1885 when Mother was eighteen. At that time, she didn't seem to have encouraged him either, although she told me years later that they enjoyed each other's company on the walk round the island.

If my father was really determined about anything, he wouldn't give in and he usually got what he wanted in the end. He fell in love with my mother and was determined that she should become his wife, however great the obstacles. My grandfather encouraged other young men whom he considered to be much more suitable, but after a while Mother and Father started to meet secretly, leaving letters for each other in a hole in the wall.

Uncle Lloyd, my father's guardian, wasn't very happy about the friendship either, but apparently took a liking to Mother when he met her. After his first meeting with her, he told another member of the family, 'She has a quietly self-assured and dignified personality, with a keen sense of humour. She is not interested in worldly ambitions.'

Three years after their first meeting, Father qualified as a solicitor, and my grandparents agreed to the marriage. It took place in the tiny Pencaenewydd Chapel, on the Lleyn Peninsula not far from Criccieth, which my mother and grandparents used to attend. There was only a handful of guests at the wedding itself, but some of my parents' friends celebrated the occasion with fireworks and a bonfire that night.

They spent their honeymoon in London and returned to Mynydd Ednyfed afterwards to live with my grandparents while Father built up his practice. My older brother and sister, Richard and Mair, were both born there. After Mair was born, Grandfather decided to retire from the farm. He built a pair of houses closer to the centre of Criccieth but still overlooking the sea, and gave one of them to my parents. I was born in the house which my father named Brynawelon. My grandparents lived in the adjoining house, which was named Llys Owen.

The houses were solidly built and are still standing. All the woodwork inside was in pine, even the cellar doors. The nursery was right at the top of our house, and we had marvellous views of the sea and mountains.

Uncle Lloyd, with my cousin William (W. R. P. George).

Mother inherited both houses and later sold the house where I was born to a bank manager, but kept the other. Eventually it was given to me and my husband, Tom, and we spent many happy holidays there with our children. That was sold too after Tom retired and we moved to my present home, Eisteddfa.

Uncle Lloyd, my father's guardian, was a great favourite of mine. He lived at Garthcelyn, about a mile from our house. He was a regular visitor and we often used to go and see him at his house. I couldn't quite manage his name; I used to call him 'Cloyd'. One day I heard he was ill. I had got it into my head that he had lost the use of his legs and couldn't come and see us any more. I couldn't have been more than two-and-a-half at the time, but I was determined to go and find out for myself how he was.

As I went out through our front gate, I met a woman coming along the road. She asked me where I was going and I said in Welsh, 'Cloyd sick. Going Celyn to see him.' Off I went. When I got to Garthcelyn I was met by my aunt, who also lived there. I was quite breathless by that time after the long walk, but I managed to get out the words: 'Cloyd sick. I want to see him.'

I told her I thought he couldn't come and see us because he hadn't any legs, and I was determined to see his legs! She took me up to his bedroom and had to undo the bedclothes to show them to me. Uncle Lloyd must have been about 50 at the time, and I remember he had a beard which was outside the sheets as he lay in bed. But I wasn't at all interested in his face—I only wanted to see whether his legs were all right—and they were!

In the meantime, Mother had been looking for me all over the garden when the maid told her that I had been seen going down the road. She rushed up to Garthcelyn as fast as she could to fetch me. I remember that she was very cross with me, but all I could talk about was Uncle Lloyd's legs!

Criccieth to us in those childhood days was absolute heaven. After we moved to London, we returned for holidays every summer and at other times as often as we could, and we used to cry when we had to leave. We hated being in London. For one thing we had much more freedom at Criccieth, because there were very few cars and you could walk along the roads without any fear of being knocked over. There were so many things we could do at Criccieth which we couldn't do in London. At that time Brynawelon was the last house along the road that led to Porthmadog, apart from a farmhouse. There were green fields all around us.

From Brynawelon there were two different ways of getting to the beach. You could go a little way down the road; and then turn towards the sea down a lane with a stream running beside it. The lane led over the railway line, and probably for this reason we were always discouraged from using it. Because it was forbidden, we often sneaked down the hill to the beach this way. On the main road, which was only a lane then, there was a turnpike. Where it used to stand there is now a petrol station.

The other way to the beach, and the way we were encouraged to go, was up the road, towards the High Street. From this direction the lane to the beach went under a railway bridge, and this was thought to be a much safer way for us to go. We used to rush down to the beach with our friends to play, often returning with grazed knees and torn clothing. One day, when I was with two much bigger girls, I remember running under the bridge and falling down, cutting my knee and tearing my dress. Even now, more than 80 years later, I still have a slate-coloured scar on my knee where the loose slate from the road surface penetrated the skin.

Grandfather used to take us along the sea wall, and we loved running up and down it. There was a song he used to sing in Welsh as I ran: 'Little Olwen and I were going to London, but the way is far and the water is wet, so we are going to stay where we are.'

Over the years Criccieth has changed surprisingly little, although obviously there has been some new building, and some of the old cottages have disappeared. The old Town Hall, where Father held meetings, is still there, and The Maes—the green in the centre of the town—still looks much the same as it did when I was a child. The Memorial Hall was completed in 1922 and was opened by my father; where it stands there were two cottages which we passed on our way to Garthcelyn to visit Uncle Lloyd. An old man named Richard Hughes lived in one of them, and when I passed he always used to put his hand in his pocket and produce a sweet for me, usually covered in fluff and dirt from his pocket. Uncle Lloyd always stopped to talk to Richard Hughes as he crossed the Green. Next door to him was a girl who was at school with me; I always thought she was a very nasty girl as she used to fight with me.

We had picnics on the beach at Morfa Bychan—Black Rock Sands—and it was a great treat to go to tea at Tripp Farm, which overlooked the beach. Aunt Mary, Father's sister, who looked after Uncle Lloyd, used to take us. We walked from Criccieth along the railway line and up to the farm. We used to play on the beach until we were called up for tea, which was always a wonderful spread.

Another highlight was the New Year's Day party at Berea Chapel, the Baptist Chapel at Criccieth where Uncle Lloyd was one of the two Lay Pastors. It started in the afternoon with a grand tea of cakes and jellies, provided by the parents, and in the evening there was a concert. Uncle William George, Father's brother, would prepare the programme, consisting of recitations and short plays, entirely in Welsh. My first appearance was when I was about three, and I was lifted on to a chair to recite a little four-line verse—something about a hen and a cockerel. To my astonishment, I had to do it all over again, as an encore. I couldn't understand why. 'But I've just done it!' I exclaimed. 'Yes, but they want to hear you again,' the other Pastor, William Williams, told me patiently, and he picked me up while I recited the verse once more.

In those days, the chapel was always full for services, and people even sat on the window ledges. There was great talent in the chapel, and the concerts were highly thought of. There would be singing and solos, and plays performed by the children. The evening was usually rounded off by an amusing drama, so that we all went home on a happy note. The whole concert had been arranged by my uncle, and the rehearsals beforehand were always held at his house on Sunday afternoons before Sunday School.

Life, certainly for Mother and the children, would have been absolutely perfect if we could have spent all our days at Criccieth. But Father's career and future were in London, so inexorably that is where we had to go.

After he entered the House of Commons he was always pleading with Mother to go to London with him. Naturally he wanted her with him, but how could she have gone in those very early days with three children under the age of three? He was living in one room in Grays Inn Road, and to live there with a young family would have been an absolute impossibility. They were hard up then because my father was travelling all round the country speaking, and in those days MPs had to pay their own fares. But eventually, Father got a small flat in Kensington Palace Mansions and we moved there in 1895, when I was three. That same year my younger brother, Gwilym, was born.

Chapter II

1895—1902

GROWING UP IN LONDON

I was barely three when the family moved to London, but although I grew up there and spent a great deal of my life in or near London, I have never regarded myself as anything but Welsh. I have on occasions described myself as 'London Welsh', for we had many friends among the other Welsh exiles in London, but I always felt intensely Welsh and the Welsh language has always been of the greatest importance to me.

Indeed, Welsh was the only language I knew until I was about seven. Welsh was the language of our home, for amongst ourselves we never spoke anything else. We never had any servants who were not Welsh. There was a time, I believe, when my father became rather concerned about us children and very anxious not only that we should learn English properly but also that we should get to know and love English literature. He got into the habit of telling us stories on Sunday afternoons. He was re-reading *The Hunchback of Notre Dame* and some of the other great historical novels of the time. *The Count of Monte Cristo* and most of the Charles Dickens novels were among them.

On Sundays we would gather round in the drawing room in our house at Wandsworth Common and he would tell us the story up to the point he had reached that week. Often we got so excited over the story that someone would say, 'Oh tell us what happened after that.' Tada invariably replied, 'Well, I don't know. I haven't reached that bit yet. You'll have to wait until next week.'

Tada was a great reader and always had a book on his bed-side table, usually something which was historical or had an exciting theme.

One of my earliest memories of London was while we were living in the flat in Kensington Palace Mansions—that was No 10 too, I remember. We hadn't been there very long, because Gwilym was a baby and I was only three. Mother was going to post some letters in the hall downstairs. We were on the top floor—the fourth floor. The baby was asleep in the flat, but I couldn't be left alone, so Mother took me with her in the lift to the ground floor. She left the door open. We posted the letters, but when we came up again, I ran ahead of her into the flat while she was closing the lift gates, and the flat door slammed behind me. Mother didn't have a key.

When I was older she told me that she had pushed open the letterbox to tell me to be a good girl and stay quiet, and all she could see were two enormous blue eyes looking at her. My head just reached the letter box. 'Open the door for Mummy,' she said, but I suppose I could barely reach the knob. At any rate, I couldn't open the door. By that time I think she was getting into a frenzy, but she was still keeping calm.

'There's a key on the windowsill,' she told me. 'Go and fetch it, there's a good girl.'

I toddled off and got the key. Her fingers came through the letterbox. 'Now put the key between my finger and thumb,' she said. I did as I was told and she opened the door, to the great relief of us both. For years this was one of her favourite stories, and she used to tell all our friends how I was locked in the flat all alone.

When we were small, we were taken out every afternoon for walks along the river with our nursemaid, Kate. I remember we hated holding her hands because they were always hot. Gwilym and I used to hold one hand each. We used to go into Kensington Gardens and see a lot of other children with their nannies. I had a hoop and I loved bowling it as I skipped along the paths.

As a little girl I was mad on dolls. Of all my toys I loved the dolls best and my father often used to bring me one home when he'd been away. On one occasion he had been to Brighton, where there was a famous preacher named Campbell. The preacher asked my father, 'Have you got a little girl at home—one who likes dolls?' My father said he had, and Mr Campbell gave him a most beautiful doll for me. I remember Tada's words as he gave it to me: 'You had better take great care of it because it was very nice of him to give it to you.'

That doll quickly became my pride and joy and I was very careful when I played with it. But I had reckoned without my brother, Richard, who was always teasing me. He loved to pull dolls' eyes out of their sockets, letting them spring back again on the bit of elastic which held them there. 'You can't touch my doll!' I shouted. But he did, and the eyes wouldn't go back again. I was furious and I remember being sick with crying. I cried for days because the doll couldn't be mended.

At that time, what I wanted more than anything else in the world was a doll's pram. When I went out to play with other children, if my friends had a doll's pram I used to monopolise it. None of the other children got a look in. When my birthday or Christmas came along I used to pray: 'Please God give me a doll's pram.' But I never got one.

Tada and Mam were not well off then and I suppose they just couldn't afford to buy one. It probably did me no harm, although a great disappointment to me at the time.

As a young child, I was often sent back to North Wales to stay with my grandparents at Criccieth, because I was always getting sore throats. I had to have my tonsils out. I loved staying at Criccieth because my grandparents used to spoil me. My mother used to say I was impossible for weeks after going back home again.

My very early schooldays were at Criccieth. I went for a short time to the nursery class at the old school there. I remember the school very well. We were all together in one big room, and the scholteacher was Miss Lily Jones. She was very nice, but I remember being afraid of the headmaster, whose name was Mr Burnell. I believe he was a very good headmaster, but I held him in great awe. Little incidents from the school come back to me still. I remember having drill, although I can't really recall any of the lessons. There was a girl with long hair who came to school one day after having it cut quite short, and, when I went home, I told my grandmother that Ruth was not a girl, but a boy! On another occasion one of the children fainted. I went home that time and told them in all seriousness that the child had died at school.

While I was living with my grandparents, I used to walk to school each day with my sister, Mair, and Mattie, the little girl who lived next door. One day we set out as usual, but Mair and Mattie soon turned back and went home. They explained that they had seen a 'nasty tramp' on the way. Immediately they were asked, 'But where is Olwen?' 'Oh, she's gone on to school,' was the reply. It was true. I was quite happy, and not a bit frightened by the tramp, so on I went as usual.

Later I went to a Board School in London. I was about six then, but I still couldn't speak English. I can remember my feelings of frustration. I was a chatterbox by nature and there I was with a lot of new playmates but sadly I couldn't communicate with them. They were talking away in English—which I didn't understand—and I just had to keep quiet. I might not have been able to speak English, but I could read a bit and I knew my tables. Not being able to let people know what I could do made me very unhappy.

Eventually I couldn't stand it any longer and to everybody's surprise I burst out with a great torrent of Welsh.

By this time we had moved from the flat into a house on Wandsworth Common. My mother had always been used to having a garden, and she wanted us children to grow with space to play out of doors. Also, my father loved having people in the house and was a very good host. In a larger house we were able to have friends to stay with us, including other MPs. Friends also stayed with us during the Parliamentary recesses, when we all went back to Wales to stay at Criccieth.

When I was still quite small, I remember particularly Harold Spender—Stephen's father—coming to stay. I liked him very much. Every morning I would see him going along the corridor to the bathroom as I sat on my bed waiting for the someone to dress me. He used to shout to me from the doorway: 'Well, Olwen! And how are you today?' I used to giggle.

Mother liked being out of doors and she liked games. She enjoyed playing cricket with the boys, and sometimes sent the ball into other people's gardens. She used to send Gwilym, the youngest boy, to fetch it. Eventually we had to stop her because she was losing too many balls.

When I grew a bit older I left the Board School and went into the kindergarten at Clapham High School with my sister, Mair. It was about two miles away, but we weren't allowed to take the bus unless it was raining. We had to walk. My father was terribly keen on exercise and we used to walk a lot. Later on I was given a bicycle, which was a great joy to me, although Mair continued to walk.

Mair was always very obedient, very gentle and a very conscientious student. I was quite the opposite, and full of mischief. I played around and did as little work as I could, unless it was subject I liked, such as German.

There was no Baptist Chapel nearby, so we used to go regularly to the Welsh Methodist Chapel at Clapham Junction. This meant going in the afternoon to Sunday School, staying to tea and attending the evening service. Lallie, our maid, used to take us mostly because Mother went to the morning service.

Sometimes Father used to take us in the evening to Castle Street Baptist Chapel, which he liked to attend, but this was a long way for us to go. As we grew older, Richard and myself chose to follow Father as Baptists, but Mair, Gwilym and Megan became Methodists.

Father enjoyed listening to a good preacher and quite a number of famous preachers, many of them Welsh, of course, came and stayed with us. They included John Williams of Brynsiencyn, Anglesey. Tada had heard Spurgeon, the celebrated Baptist who founded the training college, and Kenneth Horne's father, Silas Horne, who was a famous preacher.

Father didn't make us go to chapel, but we all went because mother insisted. I think the idea of sending us to Welsh Chapel in London was mostly to keep up our Welsh.

Mother wasn't at all puritanical, but we had to observe Sunday, especially when we were staying at Criccieth with my grandparents. We were not allowed to read books or play games. We weren't supposed to get into mischief, but my brothers were awful, and used to do all sorts of dreadful things. Looking back, they weren't really so dreadful, just mischievous.

In chapel, Dick was often impossible, and we children used to choke back laughter at his antics all through the service. He was very restless, fidgeted a lot and dropped things. There would be a dreadful clatter in the middle of a prayer when he kicked a foot-rest over or dropped a hymn book.

Unlike children today, we used to entertain ourselves and make up our own games. We dressed up a lot. We had a wonderful game we called *penbwl*, which is Welsh for 'block-head'. Everybody except one had to go and hide and we used to go all over the house. We had an old tam o'shanter, and the idea of the game was that whoever had the tam o'shanter had to hunt out the others, and hit them on the head with it when they were discovered. Sometimes we played it in the garden. We had a big vegetable garden and one day while we were playing *penbwl* I saw Dick's cap among the rhubarb leaves. I thought he was hiding there, but when I went over and shouted, 'I've found you,' he jumped out from behind a tree, pounced on me and hit me with the tam o'shanter. We invented lots of games, but I think this was my favourite.

Parties were always highlights of the year and we got very excited when someone was having a birthday. Great preparations took place in the kitchen, and all our friends were invited. Lallie supervised the whole thing, and made wonderful iced cakes and pink and white blancmange. Blancmanges were vey popular in those days; we called them 'shapes'. We also had home-made lemonade, and even now I remember how delicious it was—fruity and sweet, yet with a fresh sharpness you never get in the mass-produced bottled product that children drink today. The table would be loaded with food. We all wore our best clothes and we played games after tea.

We went to Madame Tussauds and to pantomimes and, I suppose, to most of the places in London which children visited in those days. Father was very keen for us to see everything and used to take us round London himself whenever he could. He took us to the theatre quite often. He always took us out on Sundays, usually to the park, but we often went on other outings with him. I remember being taken by him to Brompton Oratory to listen to the choir. I was fascinated by the incense; it was all quite strange for a child brought up in the Non-Conformist tradition.

To go to the House of Commons was a great treat. Gwilym had great respect for the policemen there. He would go up to all the policemen he saw and shake them by the hand. My mother had told him, 'You will have to be a good boy because there are a lot of policemen at the House of Commons.' I suppose that once he had shaken their hands he thought he was quite safe!

Father introduced us to the delights of hot chestnuts and freshly baked potatoes bought from a street barrow. Sometimes, on a Sunday evening after we had been to Castle Street Chapel, he would take us all out for a meal. Usually we went to Gatti's. He wouldn't tell us where we were going until we were almost there. Father would order lamb cutlets for us, and we were allowed to order our own sweet, usually meringues, which I loved. It was a tremendous treat. At that time there were six of us. Richard was away at school and later at Cambridge, and wasn't at home very often.

During the long school holidays Father had to remain in London for at least part of the time we were at Criccieth. In his absence, Aunt Polly arranged treats for us, and one was a coach trip to Beddgelert. The coach was pulled by two horses and driven by a man named Griffiths, of the Railway Hotel, Criccieth, and the great thing was to sit on the box with him. The Beddgelert trip was a treat we all looked forward to, but on one occasion, when I was about eight or nine, I had done something which greatly displeased Aunt Polly, and to my utter horror she said I would be left behind. Off she went with Mother, Mair and Gwilym. I thought I had been very unfairly treated, for I don't suppose I had done anything terribly bad, but she was very strict. I was determined to go. I knew my uncle had a bicycle at Garthcelyn, so I went there and borrowed it. It was a man's bike, of course, with a crossbar, and it was much too big for me, but I managed to get on, and pedalled all the way to Beddgelert—a good ten miles, and a lot of it hilly. I knew where they were going to have tea, and that is where I found them. I arrived absolutely exhausted. 'Good gracious, who have we here!' Mother exclaimed. 'How did you get here?' When I told them, I think they were so impressed they let me stay for tea and go back with them on the coach. I remember feeling awfully stiff next day!

Another great treat was to go to Pwllheli. There was a tram which went along the coast from Pwllheli to Llanbedrog, where there was a lovely house called Glyn-y-Weddw, a showplace with a beautiful garden and museum, which we loved to visit. I remember coming home once and building a little path in the garden at Brynawelon. 'I'm trying to make a garden like Glyn-y-Weddw,' I told everyone.

It was, for the most part, a very happy childhood for us all, marred only by those occasions when my father's political beliefs and dedications led him to take a stand which was unpopular with the majority of the people. We soon discovered that we were getting caught in the crossfire. Things became difficult at school; we had to defend Tada, but it was not easy. Some of our friends shunned us and, worse, some of them ridiculed and jeered at us.

I was first most acutely conscious of this during the Boer War, but it was Richard who suffered most at that time. It was an awful period for us children, for my father was pro-Boer. It felt like being a traitor, but my father was quite right. We, the British, were the aggressors. Father used to attack Joseph Chamberlain, and my mother used to be terrified when he went to speak at political meetings at that time.

There was the now famous meeting at Birmingham Town Hall. Father insisted on going because he had promised and he always kept his word, however inconvenient. My mother, although she was very worried because there had been threats to kill my father, agreed he must go. It was arranged by Harold Spender that he would send a Fleet Street Runner to inform my mother of how the meeting had gone.

All the younger children, including myself, were sent to bed but Dick, who was about ten at the time, stayed up with my mother. The Fleet Street Runner arrived about midnight to say that father had escaped from the meeting dressed as a policeman. There were about 500 policemen surrounding the building that night, but the crowd broke every window. Father wasn't allowed to say a word, but at least he got away. His disguise worked, even though he was much shorter than all the other policemen. Gwilym told me afterwards, 'I wish Father was a policeman. I would much rather he was a policeman than a politician.'

At that time Dick was going to Dulwich College. Mother couldn't understand why he kept losing his cap. He always made some excuse, and for a time she accepted it, scolded him and bought him a new one. One day he burst into tears and gradually she got the true story out of him. He used to go to school by train and every time he got into the carriage with about six other boys from the school they all got on to him and threw his cap out of the window. They dared him to 'tell' on them—but of course he couldn't do that.

Mother didn't say very much when he told her, but went away and thought about it. She talked to my father, and it was decided that Dick should go back to North Wales. He lived with my father's brother, Uncle William George, at Garthcelyn, Criccieth, and went each day to the local grammar school at Porthmadog. He was very happy there and did well. Eventually he went to Cambridge.

I think my father was very brave to adhere to his convictions. At that time he had just set up an office in London to start his law practice there in partnership with a Mr Roberts. At first they did very well, but as the war went on people began to boycott his practice. Father became very worried about money, and I heard him tell my mother, 'I will have to live in an attic and you will have to go home to North Wales.' Her reply was characteristic: 'If you live in an attic I will live in it with you.' Fortunately, it didn't come to that. My uncle was very good, and ran the practice at Porthmadog. Things would have been impossible without his help.

Even those dreadful days had their lighter side. Everyone at school used to wear patriotic badges with the name of General French, the British commander, on them. Of course we weren't allowed to wear them, although we would have loved to have done so. When Mafeking fell, our house was the only one in the street which was not decked with flags. That was too much for me and my brother, Gwilym, who was then about five. We found two pennies, ran down the street to the local penny bazaar, and bought two flags. They were rather puny flags, but we were very pleased with them and promptly hung them out of an upstairs bedroom window.

Father came home from the House of Commons and stormed at my mother: 'What is the meaning of those flags?'

Mother, not quite getting his meaning, said, 'Oh yes, dear. They are everywhere.'

'But not in our house!' Father bellowed.

'There are no flags here,' Mother replied, and she didn't believe him—not until he took her outside and she saw the two pathetic flags flying from the window. 'Oh it must have been the children', she said. 'They must have been ashamed that our house was the only one without flags.'

That was one piece of naughtiness for which Father did not punish us. To his credit he saw the humour and the pathos of the occasion.

Chapter III

1902-08

SCHOOLDAYS

Throughout his political career my father was always fighting for some cause, and in his early days as a politician education was one of the causes he felt most strongly about. He desperately wanted to end the injustices of the education system as it was at the end of the last century. He wanted to open the doors of learning to all, to end a situation where education was the prerogative of the rich. He also wanted to free education from the grip of the Church, as he saw it. He recalled his own schooldays at the village school at Llanystumdwy—a church school, where even as a child he resented being compelled to bow to the dictates of church doctrine, and felt that nonconformists should be allowed their own beliefs.

He saw the education issue as part of a much wider social reform, and he also campaigned for land reform and for the disestablishment of the Church of England in Wales. Gradually, the power was taken away from the landowners and from the Church, and new secondary schools were set up all over Wales to provide the wider education which had not been available to him. Father left school at 14 because there was no money then to send him to college, and he rejoiced in the new opportunities which were beginning to open up for Welsh children.

But when Balfour introduced his Education Bill of 1902, which would bring the Church of England schools within the national education system, Father was incensed. The Bill meant that while the public at large would pay through the rates for education in church schools, the Church would continue to own the buildings, appoint managers and teach church doctrine. Very quickly Father became the main opponent of the Bill, and he was in great demand to speak at meetings all over the country. We were not very well off, but he never turned down a request to speak, often going entirely at his own expense. In one session of Parliament, he spoke 138 times on the Bill. Wherever he went, he sent postcards and letters to us at home, and particularly to Uncle Lloyd at Criccieth. However busy he was, he never failed to send his regular bulletins to Uncle Lloyd, who expected, and got, a letter from Father almost daily.

When the Bill became law, Father continued to oppose it, and the 'Welsh revolt' against church schools, as it became known, went on until the end of 1905, when the Conservative Government resigned.

Whenever Father set his mind to anything he always saw it through, and as children we never failed to recognise how hard he worked. One of his favourite remarks to us was: 'Whatever you do, do it to the best of your ability.' We always felt that he set us a wonderful example in that way.

In 1902, my youngest sister, Megan, was born. Soon after, Sarah Jones from Criccieth came to us, first as Megan's nurse and then as our housekeeper. Sarah, or Lallie, as she was called by the family, stayed with us for over 50 years. After my mother died, she stayed on and looked after Megan. I'm not certain how she got the name Lallie, but I believe it was a name made up by Megan when she was very small. At any rate, Sarah Jones was never called anything but Lallie. She was one of the old types of maid—she could do anything. She was very capable and very loyal, and used to boss us all about. Cook was absolutely terrified of her.

Lallie looked after my father as a valet would have done. She used to say to us, 'He really is impossible.' On one occasion Father said to her, 'You haven't put a handkerchief out for me.' Her reply was quite sharp: 'You haven't looked on your dressing table, sir!' Father was quite spoilt and that was the fault of his mother, who had run about for him when he was a small boy. He was always the most important one in her family and was never allowed to lift a finger himself.

The death of Grandfather Owen in 1903 came as a great blow to us all, and Father and Mother went to Criccieth for the funeral, leaving the rest of us in London. There was a letter to us from Criccieth, dated 6 November 1903, which I still have. Father wrote:

> My dearest little children,
> Your letters today gave great pleasure to us all. I hope you will continue to write to Mami. It helps her and Nain so much to bear up.
> Megan bach annwyl's letter was specially welcome. We had no idea she could write such excellent English. We knew that she was a good Welsh scholar but had no notion that she had made such progress with her English studies.
> Maggi Thomas will be there tomorrow and will tell you all about Criccieth and about Taid's funeral.
> And so you are getting fog there now are you? Dear old foggy London yntê Wil bach?

The letter continues in Mother's handwriting:

> I want you *all* to be very careful to put *matches* out of reach of Megan bach. She is very fond of playing with them and they are poisonous. I must try and go to chapel tonight to hear a sermon about poor dear Taid. I don't know how to go.
> Love to you all
> Your ever loving Mag.

Letters were always very important when any of us were apart. It was round about that time that I wrote a birthday letter to Father from 179 Trinity Road. It is dated 16 January:

Dear Tada,

I wish you many happy returns of the day. I hope you will have a nice, quiet holiday. Have you had my postcard? Maggie has had a telegram saying that Mr. Thomas was just the same and they have sent for Mrs. Thomas. It is very awkward for him there by himself. Megan bach is alright. She was saying just now 'Mae Mami?' Gwilym is playing with his fort. We are in a hurry to go to the pantomime. We are going to Shakespeare. The play is Cinderella. No more today.

With love from Olwen.

At the bottom of the letter I had written: 'Turn over,' and on the other side I had drawn a picture, labelled 'Tada Coming Home'.

The Liberal landslide of 1906 was a time of great excitement for us all. Sir Henry Campbell-Bannerman was Prime Minister, and he sent for my father. There was a Local Government Board Minister in those days, and Father said he would like that job. He didn't get it, but he sent Mother a telegram saying:

Llywydd y Bwrdd Marchnad, reit hapus. Cariad D. [President of the Board of Trade, and quite happy.]

Welsh was still the language of our home, and it was only natural for Father to send the telegram in Welsh.

I was now 14, and it was decided that I should go away to school to Dr Williams's at Dolgellau, my mother's old school. She had been one of the first pupils there. The school had a good reputation, but I don't remember very much about it because I had a bad attack of quinsy and the doctors quickly decided the damp Dolgellau air didn't suit me at all.

I was there for only about a year, not a particularly distinguished year, I think. I can't remember excelling at anything, and certainly no one seems to have kept any of my school

The family in 1905. Left to right, Olwen, Mair, Mother, Megan, Father and Gwilym. Richard was away at school.

Caernarfon, 1906, when Father received the Freedom of the Borough.

reports, although Mother still had some of hers years afterwards.

Megan and I once found one of Mother's old reports and all the subjects were described as being 'very good', except for the domestic subjects, like cooking and sewing, which were only 'fair'. She disliked cooking and sewing, although she did sometimes do embroidery or tapestry work, and we always teased her about this. Father sometimes gave her little digs about her lack of domestic skills. Once, while we were all at Criccieth, Father was looking out of the window at the sea and Mother was talking in a not very complimentary way about a woman she knew but didn't like much. Suddenly Father said to her, 'You know what people say about you, don't you? They say that you never have needle in your hand from one end of the year to the other!'

There was a deathly silence from mother until she saw my father's shoulders heaving. She said to him, 'You made that up.' He admitted he had, but what he said about her was quite true and the truth sometimes hurts!

Mother loved being in the open air and she would far rather potter about in the garden than prepare a meal. But she always took a great interest in my father's career, backing him in everything he did. She took an active part in campaigning for him at election times, particularly when, as a Minister, he had to be absent from his own constituency to speak on behalf of other candidates.

Although she was not very tall, Mother was well built, and always looked imposing. She was a head shorter than Father, who was, I recall, exactly the same height as myself—5ft. 7½ins. He was quite short-necked, but he had very good legs and calves, and I believe he was quite vain about them.

As a young man, Father had the most lovely curly brown hair, which he usually wore rather long; he was very proud of it. On one occasion, when he was in Brussels with Mother, he decided to have it trimmed. She sat on a seat in one of the gardens while he went into the barber's. Half an hour later

Father came to find her, and she was absolutely horrified, for his hair had been trimmed really close to his head. 'I told you only to let the hairdresser take a little off,' Mother said. Father was furious, too. He said, 'I told him, but he must have misunderstood. When I complained he said, "You said you wanted a leetle—so you've got a leetle..."'

Father used to say he was a very patient man. That remark would be greeted with shouts of laughter from the family, and he would say, 'No, I mean politically! I will wait forever if necessary.'

When he was dealing with industrial disputes, he used to talk to the men concerned, and listen to their point of view. In the end, when the settlement came, he used to make them believe that it had come from them.

It was while I was at Dr Williams's School that we suffered a terrible blow with the death of my sister, Mair, at the age of only seventeen. A great deal has been written since about her death and its effect on my parents. It has been dramatised on stage and television and much of this has absolutely disgusted me. My father would never have behaved in the way he was shown in the television series. That was completely out of character.

In the television story Mair was taken ill while she was giving a piano recital at our home at Routh Road, Wandsworth Common. It didn't happen like that at all. She was in the middle of studying for Matriculation at Clapham High School and was taken ill at school. She had been working very hard, but Mair was not the sort of girl who complained about things and it wasn't until she got to school that morning that she told anyone she had a pain. By this time she must have been in very great pain, for the Headmistress, Mrs Woodhouse, telephoned Mother and told her she was sending Mair home in a cab. One of the mistresses went with her. Mother called in the doctor and told him she would like to have a specialist to see Mair. The doctor said there was no need at that time, but promised to get a specialist should it become necessary.

There was a railway strike at the time and Father, who was then at the Board of Trade, had gone to Newcastle to try to settle it. He was told of Mair's illness. Her condition became worse and Mother insisted that a specialist should be brought in. When he saw Mair he said she had peritonitis, and he must operate at once—at the house because she couldn't be moved to hospital. This was just after a similar successful operation had been performed on the King.

With the help of two nurses who had been called in, Father's study on the first floor was prepared as an operating theatre. Father arrived home from Newcastle just before the operation. In the television series he is shown rushing into the room while the operation was in progress. Nothing like that happened. Although I was away at school at the time, members of the family and a close friend who were there told me later that Father remained downstairs in the drawing room all the time.

Naturally he was restless and kept asking for someone to go up and see whether it was all over. Eventually, the surgeon came down and told Father that the operation was over and Mair had come round. But alas, it was too late. She just slipped away, and her last words were: 'The Lord is merciful and wise.'

Both my parents were absolutely shattered by Mair's death. Father was outwardly terribly upset and very emotional. Mother was not the type to show her grief and bore it grimly. I didn't see her for some time immediately after Mair's death because I was at school and too ill to come home, but when I did see her I realised how deeply she felt it. It was something she couldn't share with my father. I have a letter from her saying: 'Father has gone to the House of Commons. It's terrible for him.' It was the first time he had appeared in the House since Mair's death. Mother was always comforting him, as if she didn't have the same sort of feelings herself.

As we grew up, Mair and I had become very close and her death was a terrible shock to me. I used to get letters from her at school and in one letter just before she died she wrote: 'I have been given a lovely box of chocolates which I am sending to you.'

Mair was always full of fun and had just started going out to the theatre and to parties with my parents. She was very attractive and Father liked to show her off to his friends. She was very musical and had a good piano teacher, but there was no talk of her giving recitals. She certainly wasn't good enough for that then, although she might well have been in a year or so, had she lived. She used to play for my father, particularly on Sunday nights, when a lot of the Welsh MPs came round to the house. We all enjoyed that. One of them I remember specially was Mr William Jones, MP for Caernarfon County, a bachelor; we thought he was marvellous because he always brought us sweets.

After Mair's death, Father threw himself even more into his Parliamentary work. He was always very busy at the Board of Trade. It wasn't a very important office when he took it over, but he made it more important and it played a major part in establishing him as a politician to be reckoned with. He talked to the heads of the Civil Service Departments and they used to marvel at the way he could absorb so much information in a very short time. Any problem, no matter how small, was important to him and he used to say to us: 'Little things matter. The little touches are important.'

The Christmas following Mair's death was the first we didn't spend together as a family. Father couldn't bear to be at home so he went, on the invitation of Lord Davenport, by car to the South of France, taking the boys with him. Mother, Megan and I went to Criccieth to spend Christmas with our relatives in much the same way as we had always done. Father wrote home often. In one letter which arrived on New Year's Day, he wrote a postscript: 'Hoping you'll give something to the poor at Christmas. If not, give on New Year's Day. Give more than last year—double it!'

Normally Father was a great person at Christmas. He threw himself into all the festivities, for there never were any half measures with him! We always had a big Christmas tree and there would be a turkey on Christmas Day and a goose at New Year. Usually we went to North Wales and on Christmas afternoon we used to go to Garthcelyn for tea with Uncle Lloyd, Uncle William and Aunt Mary—or Aunt Polly as we called her. She was Father's sister and was married to a sea captain, but she also looked after her Uncle Lloyd and her brother William. She spoilt us rather because she had no children of her own.

I remember vividly one Christmas being completely spoilt for me when I was about nine because the revivalist preacher, Evan Roberts, had been invited to stay with us at Brynawelon. He used to preach at meetings at Criccieth and his appearance always caused a sensation. He only had to stand there without saying a word for people to start unburdening themselves of their guilt, to vow publicly and loudly that they would never again touch drink and to make all kinds of promises. My brother Richard said Evan Roberts was 'magic' and could turn children into frogs if they misbehaved themselves. So when I learned that he was going to stay with us I was absolutely shattered. I tried to be as good as gold while he was there, and then, to my horror, I heard he was going with us to the party at Garthcelyn! The party, which I always enjoyed, was ruined for me. I was very subdued the whole time and on the way home, as we were all walking down the hill, the preacher suddenly grabbed me and asked, 'Are you happy?' 'Oh yes, yes, yes!' I replied, and rushed to my parents for safety. He terrified me! But that was in happier days.

When Father eventually returned to England with the boys we had moved into a new home in Cheyne Place,

Chelsea, leaving behind the Wandsworth Common house where we had been happy for so long, but which now had such sad memories for us all.

About the same time, we also left the house at Porthmadog Road, Criccieth, where my parents had started their married life and where I was born. By that time, both my grandparents had died, my grandfather first, followed about a year later by my grandmother, who had been living with us. The house adjoining ours where my grandparents had lived was left to Mother, who let it for a time but later gave it to me. After my marriage, it became our holiday home and my children particularly loved going there.

But as Father began to become a national figure he needed somewhere which could provide more privacy than the Porthmadog Road house. He decided to build a new one on the top of the hill, still with the same view of the castle, the sea and the mountains, but in a secluded position and shielded by trees. We took the name of our old house—Brynawelon—with us and the original house was sold. It is now known as Llys Owen. Brynawelon became a true retreat for my Father when he needed to get away from the pressures of Parliament and Government and we loved it. In years to come it became Mother's home, and after her death, my sister Megan lived there for many years.

Besides a new home I also had a new school. It was decided that I should leave Dr Williams's School at Dolgellau and my parents' choice for me was now Roedean, the girls' public school near Brighton, the South Coast resort renowned for the therapeutic qualities of its sea air. I think it was probably the sea air and their belief that it would do my weak throat good, that tipped the balance in favour of Roedean, rather than the reputation that the school was rapidly building up under the three marvellous Lawrence sisters. They were ardent Suffragettes and Father wasn't popular with them because, although he supported the cause, they thought he and the Prime Minister, Mr Asquith, were not moving fast enough.

One day when he visited me at Roedean one of the mistresses, a keen Suffragette, rushed forward as he was leaving and leapt on to the running board of his car. 'What are you going to do about votes for women?' she yelled at him. Father was furious. 'That's the last time I shall come and see you at school,' he told me. The mistress was severely reprimanded, of course, but later on she and I became great friends. She was a very interesting woman and a marvellous teacher of English.

Roedean was an excellent school and the idea some people had that the curriculum was games and nothing but games was all wrong. It was a very healthy school in every way and the education was first class. The Headmistress was Miss P. L. (Penelope) Lawrence and her sister, Miss Millicent Lawrence, was the Second Mistress and my Housemistress. The third sister, Miss Dorothy Lawrence, was head of another school house. Roedean always had a sort of aura about it—it was considered rather a 'posh' school—and there was a story going about in those days that every girl had her own maid. I believed this and when my parents told me I was to go to Roedean I thought: Good! I've never had a maid of my own! But when I got there I soon found that, far from having a maid, you had to do everything yourself! They were extremely strict about this.

We always seemed to be changing our clothes or our stockings or our shoes. We wore white on Sundays, which made us all look lovely in Chapel, and we wore tussore dresses in the summer. But for most of the time we wore those awful djibahs, a loose-fitting garment with a blouse underneath. We hated them. When you knelt down for prayers the bottom of the skirt just touched the ground. Normally we wore black stockings in school, but every time we went out we had to change into brown stockings. By the time my daughters went to Roedean the uniform had become much more attractive, I'm glad to say.

While I was at Roedean our school subjects covered just about everything you can think of, including wood-carving. I made a little revolving bookcase, which later I gave to my brother, Richard. I was quite good at English and History and also German, which I liked, although I disliked the German teacher. I hated the mathematical side and if I didn't like something I didn't try very hard. I remember the mathematics mistress saying to me very sarcastically one day: 'Olwen Lloyd George, here's your father coping with the finances of the country and you cannot add two and two together!'

After that I thought I had better try a bit harder. Next week the mathematics teacher stood again in front of the class, with her eyes just above the top of a book—I can see her standing there now—and she said: 'You will all be very surprised to know that this week the top girl is Olwen Lloyd George!' I had got to the top by sheer hard work, but how I hated maths!

So far as games were concerned, I don't believe I was very good at any of them except lacrosse, which I loved. Discipline at the school was very good, but life seemed one long rush, with no time to do anything very much for yourself. There was a rush after breakfast every day because we had to change our black stockings for brown ones to go out and play before lessons began. Then we came back indoors and changed back into black stockings for the lessons. Looking back, it seemed an awful waste of time and effort and I cannot imagine why we had to do it.

While I was at Roedean my parents had a house at Brighton, and I used to be allowed to go home sometimes on Sundays. On one dreadful occasion I went for a walk along the sea front with Megan, who insisted on taking a doll with her. It was an enormous doll, very ugly and stood about two feet high. It was called Ceridwen and that's a name I've hated ever since. I knew perfectly well what would happen—that Megan would soon get tired and I would have to carry the wretched thing! There I was, wearing my school uniform and carrying that awful doll. I was quite sure all my schoolfriends out with their parents would see me and laugh.

I was at Roedean for only about two years, but I loved it there and made friendships which have lasted throughout my life. Two of my friends are, like me, in their nineties and we still enjoy talking over the old days. Sometimes it surprises me that I made any friends there at all, because Father was very strict and on several occasions refused to allow me to stay with girls I knew at school. I was asked to join parties for holidays abroad and I was terribly upset and embarrassed when he refused to let me go. I desperately wanted to go, but I had to make excuses and pretend I had something else to do because I couldn't bring myself to say it was Father who wouldn't let me go. I am sure I lost many friends because of that.

Father addressing some of the 40,000 miners who gathered to hear him speak about the Insurance Act at Sutton-in-Ashfield.

There were times, too, when I wasn't very popular because of things Father was doing in Parliament. When the National Insurance Act went through, there was a lot of opposition from the wealthier people. Many of the girls at school came from wealthy homes and got very cross about it, because they thought the Act was costing their fathers a lot of money. I used to feel quite sorry for them.

My father received a lot of abusive letters but there was, of course, another side to the coin. People who were benefiting from the Act showed their gratitude to him by sending all kinds of presents, many of them hand-made. Some of them were things they said they had made with their first week's pension. I still have a chair which one man made and several other things, including a tray cloth which was given to my mother at that time.

By this time we had moved from Chelsea into Number 11 Downing Street. Six months after moving into Cheyne Place, Father was appointed Chancellor of the Exchequer. Although, of course, Mother was pleased about the appointment, she was absolutely furious over the prospect of moving once more. She loved the Chelsea house which was compact and modern, and the dark, dingy corridors at Number 11 daunted her. She hated moving and you couldn't really blame her, because three moves in one year were really too much for anyone.

Chapter IV

1908-13

NUMBER 11 DOWNING STREET

Much as Mother disliked Number 11 at the outset, she soon turned it into a home for us all, and we lived there very happily for eight years, until Father became Prime Minister and we moved next door. But the first impressions of Number 11 were of a dark, depressing place with cavernous rooms which the sun scarcely penetrated, although the reception rooms all faced the back garden, which pleased my mother. Lallie was as horrified as Mother, and when she saw the vast battery of cooking utensils in the enormous kitchen—all filthy—she exclaimed in Welsh: 'My God! What am I going to do with that lot?'

The first thing was to clean everything, and introduce white paint and brighter colours. By the time I got home from Roedean for the school holidays, the transformation had taken place. Furniture had been moved around and old furnishings replaced, and everywhere was clean. There was at last an air of graciousness and comfort about the old house which it had not seen for many years. The previous Chancellor, Mr Asquith, never lived there and the house had been let. The state the tenant had left it in was absolutely unbelievable! There were magnificent views of London from the windows, and once Mother had coped with the interior it became a wonderful house in which to live.

Number 11 was part home and part offices, and more than anywhere else we had lived it was 'open house' to everyone. Cabinet colleagues, civil servants, fellow MPs and visitors of all kinds were always with us, and Mother had to organise extra meals almost daily, and at very short notice. Usually, when Father pressed a visitor to stay for a meal, she was equally anxious to offer hospitality. There was one occasion when she did not back Father with her usual enthusiasm. The visitor was Herbert Samuel, a Cabinet colleague. He and Father had been talking for some time, and lunchtime was approaching.

'You'll stay to lunch, of course,' my Father said to Herbert Samuel, who politely but firmly declined, making some excuse that he had to leave. Father turned to Mother for support. 'He must stay to lunch. We won't take a refusal, will we?' said Father. But to his surprise Mother did not try to persuade our guest to stay. Out of the corner of her mouth she said, in Welsh, 'It's pork for lunch today.' She knew well that Herbert Samuel was a strict Jew and would have been highly embarrassed to have been faced with something he could not possibly have eaten. The truth dawned on Father and he instantly stopped being the pressing host. 'Oh well, another time perhaps,' he said.

This was one of the many occasions when the Welsh language was extremely useful as a means of private communication amongst us. During the war, we often used Welsh for telephone conversations and letters, which defied all censorship because nobody could understand them.

Welsh was still very much the language for our home, and all the maids at Number 11 were Welsh. Many of our visitors were Welsh, and below stairs Lallie acquired a reputation as a tremendous host in her own right, holding court to many of her friends from North Wales. Visiting Number 11 and Lallie was a 'must' for Criccieth people when they came to London; in their eyes it was probably given higher priority than seeing Buckingham Palace or Tower Bridge! Lallie loved showing her friends round the house, pointing out the various landmarks from the windows and telling them all the various items of news.

Father would entertain people at all hours of the day, and at Number 11 became very fond of inviting people to breakfast. This was absolute agony for us children, because when we were home he expected us to be there punctually at 9 a.m.—not a minute late! He was the most punctual person in the world, not at all like Mother, who seemed to think time didn't exist. Like her, Megan was also terribly unpunctual, and as she grew older she was always late for appointments or missed trains. The family could tell many funny stories about Megan's lateness. There was one occasion when she was due to catch a train from Euston to speak in her Anglesey constituency, but the train had started to leave the platform as she rushed through the barrier. One of my sons was with her, and somehow managed to push her into the guard's van, throwing the suitcases in after her as the train steamed out.

I am by no means as fanatical over punctuality as my Father was, but Megan used to drive me to distraction sometimes. There was one occasion when I arranged to meet her in Piccadilly, outside Swan & Edgar's store. I waited for what seemed like hours, becoming more and more embarrassed by the glances of passers-by, and still she didn't appear. Eventually I got so fed up that I went home and told her that I would never arrange to meet her in the street again!

Another incident which amused us happened some years later, after I was married, and it was one which proved infuriating for my husband, Tom. My two sons, Robin and Benjy, were due to return to school after holidays in North Wales, and because the family car was temporarily out of action we hired a taxi to go to Afon-wen Station, where the boys and I were to catch a train.

The taxi, a terrible, rackety old car, arrived, driven by an old Irishman named Riley, whom we knew well. We had to go and say goodbye to my sister Megan, who was at Brynawelon, so we all got into the car and called there on the way. The boys got into a long conversation with their aunt, and my husband became frantic. 'Hurry up, Benjy, we'll miss the train!' he called. But Benjy was expecting to be given half-a-crown by his aunt, and was determined not to leave without it. And Megan kept on talking.

Eventually he got his pocket money, and off he went, but the inevitable happened, and the train was just leaving as we got to the station. 'Ah, Jesus, there she goes!' exclaimed Riley.

Tom told him to drive as fast as he could to Chwilog, the next station along the line. Again it was: 'Ah, Jesus, there she goes!' from Riley, as we saw the trail of smoke disappearing down the track at Chwilog.

By this time Tom was in a rage because he had arranged to go fishing and he absolutely hated being late for anything. He quickly made up his mind what we should do next. 'I'm going back,' he said. 'You can wait for the next train. I suggest you go for a nice walk, and have your lunch while you are waiting.'

The next train was not due for nearly three hours, but we were lucky because it was a lovely day and we had a picnic basket with us, intending to have a packed lunch on the train. The three of us quite enjoyed ourselves, and in due course the boys got back to school at Rottingdean. But once again we all blamed poor old Megan!

That was long after the Downing Street days. While we were at Number 11 Megan was involved in what now seems a highly-amusing incident, but at the time it horrified us. Megan would have been about six at the time, and was very friendly with young Anthony Asquith, the Prime Minister's son, who later became a film producer. Anthony, who was known as 'Puffin' in those days, being the boy next door and about Megan's own age, used to come round to play, and the two of them had wonderful games of hide-and-seek all over the house. Like all children they were mischievous and got up to all kinds of pranks.

One day, the two of them went missing. Some time passed, and they still failed to turn up, so the staff started a systematic search. There were fears that they might have got stuck in the lift. It was lunchtime, and Father had a luncheon party of quite important guests. The meal progressed, when suddenly someone happened to look up through the glass cupola above the dining-table. There was a narrow gallery running round the cupola, and two small figures were seen creeping stealthily along the ledge. They had climbed out of a window to get on the roof, and were intending to walk over the roof to Number 10, and climb in through another window there.

We thought that any minute one of them would slip and crash through the glass dome on to the dining-table! Luckily it didn't happen. One of the family made an excuse to leave the table, and the children were quietly and gently removed from the roof. Father's wrath afterwards was quite predictable, and needless to say that was the end of Puffin as a playmate for Megan!

At home with Megan, 1910.

Megan was a delightful child, pretty, intelligent, lively and full of fun, but thoroughly spoilt by all the family. Father was the worst culprit, and loved taking her out with him and showing her off. When she was in the middle of her lessons, he would suddenly go into the schoolroom and tell Megan's governess to get her ready, because he wanted to take her somewhere. Megan loved all that, and got quite conceited over all the attention she was getting. When I came home from school one day she said, 'I am in the papers much more than you are!' I used to tell her that criminals also got their names in the papers. I was never jealous of Megan, because I was extremely fond of her, and the only time I really became annoyed and irritated with her was when she asked me to do something which I considered to be absolutely stupid—like carrying that silly doll at Brighton when I was wearing my school uniform!

Megan would have made a wonderful actress. As a child she was always acting, and some of the distinguished visitors at Number 11 got full benefit of her performances. There was one occasion when someone called for breakfast, and the door was opened to him by the funniest little person in an apron and cap your ever saw. 'Hello,' said the visitor, 'who are you?' 'I'm the maid,' said Megan, showing him into the library, where she lingered to have a chat with him. 'Do you have to get up very early?' the visitor enquired, and Megan gave him a heart-stirring account of all the household jobs she had been doing that morning.

There was another time when she introduced herself to a visitor as Miss Evans, my Father's secretary. Father treated it all quite seriously, and sometimes used to say, 'We must ask my secretary.' The rest of us thought it was rather a joke. I remember that Megan was absolutely marvellous in school plays. She really enjoyed acting.

Father couldn't remember names, and was always getting them wrong. Some of my friends were terrified of him, and at first reluctant to come to the house because they thought he was so clever that he was on an entirely different level from them. But when they met him they used to say how much they liked him. He was a very good listener, and a wonderful conversationalist, and however shy my friends were to begin with, he soon had them talking, and always wanted to know what they planned to do with their lives.

When we were all together, talking round the table, he sometimes used to bang the top with his fists, and shout: 'Order, order!' We all stopped talking at once, and he would say, 'What I want to know is, what are we going to do this afternoon?'

When he went out on family expeditions, it was Father who led the way. He always wanted to be the *ceffyl blaen*—the leading horse—and he would go striding off, until somebody shouted: 'Hey—slow down!' Then he would walk a bit more slowly, but only for a minute or two, and then he would be off again.

Mother had a habit of walking round the house before breakfast in her nightgown, without putting on her dressing gown, much to the family's annoyance. We were always telling her that she might meet someone, and cause embarrassment. It was just the same when she got to Number 11, and one morning she came out of the bathroom, still in her nightgown, and rushed straight into the Master of Elibank, who was Chief Whip and was staying with us at the time. He was rather a large man, with a very prominent stomach. She literally ran into him, putting her hands up to stop herself. She told us she bounced off him, and ran. I think he was probably more embarrassed than she was, but it certainly didn't cure her.

She was usually up early, and I remember once at Criccieth when she was hovering round the back door particularly early. There was a tap on the door, and when she opened it there stood 'Memorial' Jones, so called because he used to look after the cemetery. Hidden beneath his coat was a large Dwyfor salmon. Father loved salmon, and

'Memorial' Jones had promised Mother he would get her one. I suspect we often got our salmon in this way.

In the Cabinet Room one day, Father was talking about hydrangeas to Sir William Harcourt. Coming from North Wales, Father naturally knew a lot about them, and there was nowhere that hydrangeas grew more prolifically or were a deeper blue in colour. Harcourt complained that his hydrangeas always turned pink. How, he asked Father, could blue hydrangeas be encouraged to keep their colour?

Father told him, 'The answer lies in the soil. What you want is some slate in it. I'll send you some slate chippings from Blaenau Ffestiniog, and you can put it round them.'

Harcourt thought it an extremely generous gesture, and thanked him gratefully. A few days later, after Father had presented his first Budget, Harcourt told him, 'I don't think you need bother to send the slate now. That Budget of yours is going to turn everything blue!'

We had been at Number 11 for about a year when I left Roedean and came home to live. It was decided that I wouldn't go to college, but while Father made up his mind about what I should do next I went with a friend who was staying with us to a cookery school in Buckingham Palace Road. Everybody thought we were going to classes when we set out, but I'm afraid we often took the opportunity of freedom the classes provided to play truant and go off on our own. Father was always very strict about where we were going, how long we would be, and who we were with, and I believe it was this attitude that made me deceitful. Anyway, we did attend quite a few of the classes, and learned something, if not very much, about cooking, and the whole thing was great fun.

We weren't prepared for what happened when Father suddenly announced that some friends were coming to dinner the following week, and we were to cook the meal. We were terrified, and quite sure the meal would be a complete fiasco. Cook had been warned not to give us any help, and there we were, completely on our own. The evening passed for us in a haze of anxiety and hard work, but somehow we produced a meal which was, at least, quite eatable. The beef was perhaps a little underdone, but the food disappeared. I had written a menu with a little verse on it which was a parody of the famous hymn 'Now the day is over'. Afterwards, Father wrote his own verse in reply:

Now the meal is over
We sigh with longing grief
For the mealy taties—
And the bloody beef!

About the time I left school Father acquired a new interest—camping. My brother Gwilym, who was then about sixteen, had been camping at school, and Father, who was very keen on outdoor life because he thought it was healthy, decided that we should all try it. Mother hated the idea, and I don't think the rest of us—apart from Gwilym—

A family camping expedition in North Wales. Father is reclining in the centre of the picture. Mother and Megan are to the left of the picture, Gwilym and myself to the right.

were very enthusiastic. We were at Criccieth at the time, so there were plenty of places not far away where we could go. Father chose Cwm Ystradllyn, a rather wild area on a plateau between Moel Hebog and the Tremadog Rocks. It was only five or six miles from home, but it could have been several hundred miles away. Tents were pitched near the lake, and we carted a vast amount of food and equipment with us, including an oil stove. Since Father didn't really believe in roughing things too much we also took a maid with us! That horrified Gwilym. 'This isn't camping,' he said.

Unfortunately we didn't have a very good weather, and I can't say we really enjoyed the experience. I think we had two nights there, and that was quite enough for us all. Father told us, 'You are an unsporting crowd!' and drove us home. He liked us to do things together as a family, and I think he visualised spending a few days away from everything in an idyllic setting, with us all going out on the lake by boat, fishing and picnicking. As it was, I think we all got rather bad-tempered, and the whole thing was not an experiment we wanted to repeat.

Having left school, I was beginning to feel grown up, and at Number 11 had for the first time my own room, where I could entertain my friends. Father still supervised my friends very carefully, and I used to have rows with him because he wouldn't let me join parties of friends who were going to Scotland or abroad. I thought I was missing all the excitement in life, and at times I did feel very resentful.

There was, however, the compensation of living in Downing Street, where everything was happening and everybody who was anybody came to visit us. Father worked hard, and often went away on fact-finding trips abroad, as well as going to meetings all over the country. He was determined to improve life for the poor and under-privileged, and when he heard how efficient the German social system was he went there to find out for himself. Even then he was aware of military activities in Germany, which made him uneasy, although, like his Cabinet colleagues, I don't think he was expecting war at that time.

Father was very close to Winston Churchill, who was then a Liberal, and Churchill spent a short holiday with us at Criccieth before his marriage to Clementine Hozier at St Margaret's, Westminster.

I still have a letter which Churchill wrote to Father on 3 August 1910, accompanying a small gift. It was written on Home Office notepaper in typical Churchillian vein. He wrote:

> My dear David,
> Here is the chain I promised to give you. May you long wear it, with the pencil of inspiration at one end, and the keys of power at the other.
>   Yours ever,
>   Winston S. Churchill.

I often went to the House of Commons to listen to the debates from the Strangers' Gallery. Before a speech, whether it was in the House or outside it, Father always became extremely tense and nervous. His stomach became upset, and he was often physically sick. He also used to perspire so much that his clothes would be wet through, and he would have to change everything. Once when I accompanied him to a function where he was to speak, he said to me, 'I'll give you £1,000 if you'll make this speech for me.' He absolutely refused to be calmed down beforehand, but once on the platform he was a different man.

When he delivered his first Budget speech in 1909, I was there in the Gallery with Mother to listen to him. His speech as he presented 'The People's Budget', as it was known, lasted over four hours. We realised what a tremendous ordeal it was for him. His taxation proposals, including new land taxes, were fought bitterly, and it was a highly emotional occasion. His statement that the Budget was for 'raising money to wage implacable warfare against poverty and squalidness' might have endeared him to the under-privileged, but the landowners and the wealthy were furious, and overnight he made many new enemies.

Under stress, Father's voice was apt to break, and throughout his Parliamentary career he had to be careful. He had an operation on his tonsils, a highly dangerous operation for an adult at that time, and was much better afterwards. But much of his trouble was, I suspect, due to nerves.

In the event, the Lords rejected his Budget, and Father became one of the most hated men of his day. Cartoonists had a glorious time, and one depicted him as a highwayman. He was called names—liar, thief, brigand and anarchist were bandied about without a second thought, but probably the favourite among the newspapers was 'Welsh poacher'. Father just battled on, and the Budget eventully went through, although it took a year and a threat that the Government would create so many new Liberal peers that the House of Lords would be swamped and all opposition would be out-voted.

One incident which Father greatly enjoyed happened when Ernest Shackleton, the explorer, called at Number 11, asking for financial help for his 1912 expedition. Like so many other visitors he came to breakfast to discuss it. Father told him reluctantly that he was sorry he was unable to provide money from Treasury funds, but he gave Shackleton the addresses of City bankers and others he thought might help. He told the explorer, 'Come back and tell me how you get on.'

Some time later Shackleton did come back, and told Father he had been very successful in obtaining money. Then he added, 'They said that if I were to take you with me they would double the contribution. And if I were to leave you in the Antarctic they would treble it!' Father was always amused by this story. He said, 'I always knew I wasn't very popular in the City, but I never knew quite how unpopular.'

King Edward VII died while we were at Number 11, and
we were all invited to watch the funeral procesion from the
windows of the Foreign Office. It was a solemn and memorable occasion, and also one of the last occasions before the
1914-18 War when the heads of European states were seen
together. The Kaiser and the King of Spain were among
those who came to pay their homage, and we gazed down on
them from the windows in awe.

About this time I became an avid autograph-hunter. With
so many eminent visitors to my home it wasn't surprising
that I should take the opportunity of getting a signature from
them before they left, and Ernest Shackleton was one of
them. Over the years at Number 11 and, later, at Number
10, I collected scores. They ranged from Harry Lauder, who
kindly wrote: 'For a Bonnie Lass', to Marshal Pétain and
the Chinese delegation to the Peace Congress of 1919—Dr
Wellington Koo, Chengting T Wang and Suntchou Wei.
Politicians, actors, preachers and anyone whose name was
the slightest bit well-known were persuaded to sign for me,
and on one occasion, on 13 February 1917, the entire
Cabinet obliged.

In 1910 it was decided that I should go to Germany for a
year. I had always enjoyed German lessons at school, and at
Roedean I had acquired a good basic knowledge of the language. So off I went to Dresden to perfect it under the guid-
ance of Fraulein Kraatz and Frau Krauss, who kept a small
establishment in Schnorstrasse for half a dozen girls at a
time. It was a very large flat, and we all had our own rooms.
Our two tutors were very kind to us, and I remember we had
very good food. I enjoyed the food so much that I'm sure I
came home twice the size I was when I went to Germany. To
start with I was so homesick that I seriously thought of
taking the next train home—the only thing that stopped me
was the realisation that I would be sent straight back again.

Our two German guardians were good disciplinarians, and
all our outings were very much controlled. We were not

allowed to go out as we pleased, and it was understood that we did not go home for holidays. We were taken on guided tours of all the places they thought we ought to see, museums, galleries—even the famous Meissen porcelain factory. We also went to the opera, and one thing which has stayed with me all my life has been an understanding and love of Wagner's work. We saw the whole of *The Ring,* and we attended lectures on the Wagner operas, so that I became quite knowledgeable on the subject.

The war was still a long way off, but we were aware of military activities. When we were taken out to a restaurant there were usually men in uniform there too. Dresden then was a most beautiful city, and the devastation during the 1939-45 war made me feel desperately sad.

While I was in Germany, letters from home were very important, and every now and again there was even one from my Father. He wrote from Balmoral Castle on 9 September 1910:

My dearest Llwydyn,

Here I send you a sprig of heather little Princess Mary gave me on the afternoon walk today with the Queen. We had quite a jolly afternoon. I was in the Queen's carriage. We walked through the forest—then the little Princess wanted to throw pieces of wood into the river. She and I got hold of a big one, and there was the greatest fun in sending it over the waterfall, the Queen shrieking with delight when I got it off after it had stuck on a stone mid-stream, and the little Princess jumping with joy. We had tea at a cottage and then drove home.

Love to you,
Yours Tada

And here is another which I received a few months later.

RMS Omrah
Friday Feb 9th 1911

My dearest Llwydyn,

I have for days projected a letter to you. At last Piggie [Megan] brought me this sheet of paper as I lay on my deck chair and she and I mean to fill it.

We have had a great time at Naples. Not what the doctor would call a restful time such as he prescribed. We have been to Pompeii—we visited Pozzuoli. (Pictrolio it is called in Acts of Apostles). Here Paul landed on his way to Rome. We launched at Baiai, the site of the old Roman watering place. You can now see everywhere ruins of old patrician villas. We passed the Mare Monto (??), the docks of the Roman fleet. We visited the ruins of Cursia—passed Lake Avenico. You recollect the old Roman tag ...

It was the old 'Llyn yn llosgi o dân a brwmstan' for being the crater of a volcano up till recent times the fumes of sulphur were exhaled from the lake and no living thing could approach it. We saw Solfatara, a crater which is hardly extinct for the hot sulphur smoke almost stifled us and there were holes broken in the muddy crust at the bottom of which a foetid water boiled and bubbled. Dwdsyn (Megan) was more impressed with this than with anything else she saw on the whole journey.

What pleased her most however was that we met two girls of your age whom I knew. One of them was exactly like you—we all said so. Piggie took a great fancy to her. When you return you and we must meet.

My throat is clearing well but my chords will be tender for some time yet.

I always derive great pleasure from reading your letters.

Love to you Llwydyn bach,

Tada

Another letter from Father came from the Treasury Chambers, Whitehall, on 24 February 1911:

My dearest Llwydyn,

Druan o Llwydyn Llwyd yn cwyno nad ydy wedi derbyn . . . I am a poor substitute, Llwyd bach, but your appeal touched me, and as your Mother is at Brighton I thought I would write to tell you we have not forgotten you. You are always in our minds, and form a constant subject for very affectionate conversation.

Piggie is upstairs and is rigging herself up for a walk with me in the Park. Tomorrow we both of us go to Brighton together to join your Mother.

Tonight I dine with the King at Buckingham Palace.

Things are going very well for the Liberals in the country and in the House of Commons. The Tories are quarrelling badly amongst themselves and are quite beaten.

If you are not back by the Coronation we must get you to the Investiture at Caernarvon, the middle of July.

I am so glad you are working hard and that you are getting such an adept in German. I am also specially keen about your music. I want you to play well, Llwyd bach. That would please me so much.

Off now to the House of Commons. I am in charge today.

Fondest love,
Tada.

A hastily written note came on black-edged Treasury Chambers notepaper on 20 April 1911:

My dearest Llwydyn Llwyd,

If you want to join the Berlin trip you had better do so. Hope you will enjoy it.

Working up a great scheme of National Insurance on German lines.

Love,
Yours Tada.

Father was obviously very much occupied with Parliamentary affairs at that time, and letters were brief. Mother

received one, also on black-edged notepaper, this time from
Number 11 Downing Street, and dated simply 'Monday',
which read:

> My Darling Mag,
> Cabinet and conferences afterwards taken up all my
> time—so cannot write. Elibank and I returned today. Golf
> Saturday and motoring yesterday.
> Shall write Dick tonight. Dining tonight with Grey,
> Haldane and Winston.
> Very satisfactory Cabinet.
>
> > Fondest love,
> > Dei.

I did get home in time for the Investiture of Prince Edward
as Prince of Wales, on 13 July 1911, a glittering occasion at
Caernarfon Castle and one which was charged with a great
deal of emotion for all Welshmen. It was a considerable
triumph for Father, who had worked extremely hard beforehand to ensure that everything would go off well, and that
Welsh suscepitibilities were not offended. For months
beforehand Father gave the Prince Welsh lessons so that he
would easily be able to make the responses in Welsh at the
ceremony, and quite a deep bond formed between the two of
them. The Prince was rather shy, and Father thought he was
a very nice young man. The Prince in his turn, seemed genu-
inely grateful to Father, and was desperately anxious to make
a good impression on the Welsh people.

After it was all over, the Prince wrote to my father from
Buckingham Palace:

> Dear Mr Lloyd George,
>
> I thank you most sincerely for all the trouble you have
> taken to make my Investiture a success. I thought that the
> ceremony was a very beautiful one. I was much touched
> by the warmth of my reception. All the Welsh people that
> I came across were very nice and kind. It was chiefly due

Father with Prince Edward, about the time of his investiture in 1911 as Prince of Wales.

to the valuable lessons you gave me in Welsh that the answers to the addresses were such a success. I really did feel what I said. The singing I heard on board the yacht was beautiful and truly 'gave me great delight'.

I am going to send you a photograph as soon as possible, as a remembrance of July 13th. Again thanking you for your kindness.

I remain,

Yours very truly,

Edward P.

Lord Stamfordham, the King's Private Secretary, also wrote Father a letter of thanks from Buckingham Palace:

Dear Lloyd George,

Having now completed his 'Progresses' the King cannot close what has been a most eventful and happy chapter in his reign without once more expressing his gratitude for all that you did in connection with the installation of the Prince of Wales at Caernarvon.

For His Majesty more than realises that both in the conception of the idea and in carrying it into effect yours was the directing mind—with the result that within those historic walls, of which you are the responsible custodian, was enacted a ceremony unique in its national character, historical in its Rites, beautiful in every detail, and the incidence of which stirred the hearts of all who were so fortunate as to be there.

His Majesty not only thanks you, but offers you his hearty congratulations upon the brilliant success of what it is safe to assert will be recorded as a memorable event unprecedented in the national life of Wales.

Believe me,

Yours very truly,

Stamfordham

After the Investiture it was decided that I should go to Paris for a year to polish up my French. There were more girls than in Germany, and we spoke more English amongst ourselves, but the French I learnt came in very useful later. Even as I left for France, Father's unpopularity with certain sections followed me. Waiting with Mother on the platform at Victoria Station, I heard one of the girls say, 'Lloyd George's daughter will be with us in Paris.' The response from the girl's mother was an immediate warning: 'Whatever you do, don't have anything to do with her!' As it

A Budget Day picture of Father.

happened, we got on very well together, and became great friends.

From time to time I heard news from Number 11, where Father was still fighting taxation battles and trying to push the National Insurance Bill through the House. His offer of 'Ninepence for Fourpence'—which became the slogan of the day—appealed to the workers, who, for the first time, had the prospect of guaranteed medical care at a cost of only 4d a week, but the scheme was bitterly fought by the employers, and was not liked either by the majority of doctors. Partly because of this, the Liberals became very unpopular, but luckily they did not have to put their popularity to the test at a general election. If they had done so the Conservatives might well have won, and the course of history for Father would have been quite different.

On a personal level, Father was pleased when Bonar Law took over from Balfour as leader of the Conservatives. He had always liked him, and greatly respected his ability. Bonar Law was always very reserved towards Father, and was reluctant to appear too friendly towards him. He regarded Father as being dangerous, and held the view that one should never fraternise with one's political enemies.

The letter Father wrote to him was perhaps unexpected in its contents, for Bonar Law wrote back to him on 16 November 1911, from Pembroke Lodge, Edwardes Square, Kensington:

> My dear Lloyd George. Thank you for your letter. It is even kinder than I should have expected, and that is saying a great deal.

Irish Home Rule and Welsh Disestablishment were still very much present, and there were still unexpected attacks from Suffragists to contend with. One such attack happened in December 1911 after Father had spoken at a Suffrage meeting at the Caxton Hall. Mother and I were with him, and were in the carriage afterwards when a despatch box

Father, with T. P. O'Connor, centre, the Irish Liberal MP who was greatly involved in the Irish question. The picture, taken at Walton Heath, also includes Mother, left, and, on the grass, Richard and Megan.

with steel corners was thrown through the window at Father, just missing his eye and grazing his cheek. I was sitting near the window as it flashed past my face. Later Father had a letter from a prominent Suffragette, Mrs M. G. Fawcett of 2 Gower Street, which read:

My dear Mr Lloyd George,

I was deeply grieved to see in today's papers that you were the victim of a cowardly assault after you had spoken at the great Suffrage meeting on Saturday. It makes me bitterly ashamed that any man calling himself a Suffragist should perpetrate such a mean and brutal outrage. I hope most earnestly that your injuries are not serious. I hope I may at the same time say how thankful I was that your daughter at once did the right and womanly thing of placing herself at the window of the carriage so as to protect you from further attack. Please thank her for all of us women who are working steadily for Suffrage and detest violence.

I take this opportunity of thanking you and Sir Edward Gray for the splendid speeches, and of expressing the hope that you will speak for Suffrage as often as possible. Men in your position speak, not merely to an audience, but to the whole nation, and every time you speak you add greatly to the great band of Suffragists throughout the country.

Even though he became so worked up before making a speech, Father thoroughly enjoyed a political meeting and welcomed hecklers. He used to scribble notes all the while, and I have kept some of these. There was one scribble in pencil at a meeting at Bedford on 11 October 1913, where he opened his campaign over land reform. One note says cryptically: 'Bedford. Don't like your politics', probably a reference to the Duke of Bedford. Another says: 'I am out to help the under-dog. I shall be deterred by no calamity.' Acland is another name pencilled there. There is also a

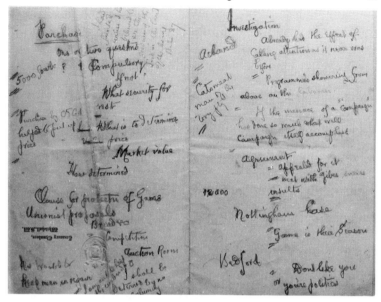

Father's jottings for his speech at Bedford on October 11, 1912, at the first meeting in the Land Campaign.

Biblical quotation from Psalm 27: 'I had fainted unless I had believed to see the goodness of the Lord in the land of the living.'

By this time I was living at home once more, and was able to accompany Father to meetings. I often went to the House of Commons, but although I was exhilarated by the political scene I never had any ambitions myself to go into politics. It never entered my head that I should, although Gwilym and Megan were both set for a political career from very early on. Another thing I could never bring myself to do was to attend an election count. I just couldn't bear the thought that Father might not win, so I stayed at home until it was all over.

That last year before war broke out in 1914 seemed a wonderful year, full of excitement and parties. We were always doing something or going somewhere, and we of the younger generation seemed to be living for the enjoyment we could get out of it. It was almost as if we knew that some of us did not have much longer to live.

But we were still a long way from the permissive society, and Father, Victorian in his attitudes, still kept a tight rein, certainly on my activities, and did not approve of too many late nights. I had to ask his consent before going out, and I was only allowed to go if he approved of my escort. I had to be in at the time he decided, which often meant leaving before the end—worse still, sometimes before the last waltz. I could go out escorted by one or other of my brothers, and there was one memorable occasion when I went with them to the Chelsea Arts Ball, a famous occasion in London on New Year's Eve, when it was fashionable to shed all inhibitions and dance into the small hours. We had a splendid time and came home very happy. Tiptoeing upstairs at Number 11 at 5 a.m. I completely forgot that one stair near the top creaked. My brothers, who were much more used to creeping in in the early hours of the morning than I was, got upstairs safely, but I, like an idiot, stepped on the creaky stair and woke Father. Next morning there was an inquest over breakfast, and I had to own up that it was me coming home at what he regarded as a disgusting hour. He was very cross, and as a punishment insisted that I spent the next evening at a Salvation Army pageant at the Albert Hall.

Chapter V

FATHER AND MOTHER

Although it was not until after I married that Mother ever mentioned Father's infidelities to me, I was aware from an early age that there were other women in his life. I was an outspoken child, and for that reason the grown-ups tried to keep things from me because I was apt to put my foot in it! I did this rather dramatically when I was about eight or nine, and Father was showing us children a gift he had just received. The incident is still vivid in my memory, even though I cannot remember what the present was; it was something quite small, like a pencil or an ornament to hang on his watch chain. Father said, 'It was given to me by a lovely lady—guess who?' The present was from Mother and obviously Father expected us to guess it quickly. We looked for clues: 'Do you kiss her?' we asked.

'Oh yes,' said Father, expecting us to say Mother without hesitation. We suggested Aunt Polly and then I dropped my bombshell.

'Was it Mrs Timothy Davies?' I asked innocently. There was the most terrible silence, and that was the first time I knew he was unfaithful.

Mrs Davies was the wife of an MP who was helped by Father, and she became his mistress. He had an enormous fascination for women, and they always went more than half way to meet his advances. Many of his friends felt he should be protected against women; they flocked round him and often threw themselves at him.

I thought Mother was marvellous although, frankly, had I been in her position I could not have tolerated his infidelities. During the time that I was growing up, she never

Even without a microphone, Father could make his voice travel a considerable distance. His is pictured at an election meeting at Criccieth.

showed us by any sign that she knew things were not as they should be, but she supported him in all his political work, particularly at election times. When she wasn't in London he used to go to Criccieth to see her, and she was always delighted to see him. Throughout the whole of their lives they retained a very strong affection for each other and I really believe that Mother always came first with him. He certainly always came first with her and when she knew he was coming to Criccieth, she did everything to please him. She was always loyal and faithful to him.

I believe Father started having affairs with other women very soon after my parents were married. Even before my brother Dick was born there was a scandal surrounding Father and another woman, and the family tacitly accepted that a son born to her was our half-brother. Whatever these affairs meant to Father at the time, most of them were little more than amorous adventures adding excitement to his life and work. They were brief, and afterwards he had nothing to do with the women concerned. When we were older we used

Father, relaxing at Criccieth.

to talk about 'Father's little peccadilloes' and there came a time when even Mother could laugh about them. Once, later in life, when some scandal had broken out concerning someone else in the public eye, I said to John Grigg, who was in the throes of writing his second book about my father, and was still looking for a title: 'Really I think it should be called St David. Even though he had all those affairs, he never did anything mean, and really the things he did were nowhere near as bad as the things done by some other politicians.'

There is no doubt that the separation when Father first went to London as a young MP put a strain on their marriage. Naturally he wanted Mother with him in London—yet how could she? By the time I was born she had three children under the age of three, and Father was still a struggling politician who could offer her very little money and only a one-room flat in London as a home.

She felt her first duty was to her children, who were infinitely better off in Criccieth, so she waited until he had found somewhere suitable for them before joining him. He missed her terribly. I have a letter which he wrote to Mother on 7 August 1901. He wrote:

'My own sweetheart. So disappointed when I got home last night not to find a wire from you awaiting me and this morning I woke up at quarter to eight and got up expecting to find a letter. Ond dim gair oddi wrth Maggie. [But not a word from Maggie.] Actually left the house at 9.30—do you think that would have happened had my round little Maggie been by my side to tumble and towzle about? Anyhow, I went to the Club, expecting letter there. Then to office. Dim yr un. [Not one.] So I left. When I came to the House of Commons I found one there. Roberts wants me to stay with him. I may on returning from Nottingham. Meanwhile write to me at House of Commons.'

The letter ends with a sentence in Welsh and is signed 'Your own Dai'.

As children, we hated seeing Mother hurt and we used to rally round her whenever Father did anything which upset her. There is no doubt that on many occasions she was deeply hurt by his behaviour. They used to try and keep things from me because they used to say I was more perceptive than the other members of the family, and I never hesitated to say what I thought.

Richard, my elder brother, was very sensitive and, even more than the rest of us, condemned Father's infidelities and the effect on Mother, although as I grew older I began to think that his attitude was affected to a certain extent by a natural jealousy for Father.

Looking back, I put a lot of Richard's naughtiness down to his concern over the relationship between our parents. Although Father always showed a lot of affection towards Mother, he also made her cry. Sometimes when she looked sad, I used to ask her if she was cross with me. 'No,' she would say, 'I'm not cross with you.' 'Then smile at me,' I urged, and she would give a little forced smile. After a time I realised it was Father who made her feel miserable. He was always very different from other fathers, and women seemed to be a necessary part of his existence. However, he always showed great affection to his own family.

Father's long-standing relationship with Frances Stevenson was in a different category, and it caused a great deal of bad feeling within the family.

Ironically, it was I who actually introduced Father to Frances Stevenson. He was Chancellor of the Exchequer at the time and had become concerned about Megan's progress at school. He decided that she should have extra tuition during the summer holidays and asked me to find her a governess, because Mother was at Criccieth. He suggested that I should approach Mrs Woodhouse, the Headmistress of Clapham High School, to see whether she knew of anyone suitable, and I also went to an agency. Mrs Woodhouse suggested Frances Stevenson might suit us. She was at the time a teacher at Allenswood School, Wimbledon, and spoke good French because her mother was French. The agency offered us a Swiss girl, and when I saw them both I greatly preferred the Swiss girl.

After I had talked to them both, Father came in. Later I asked him, 'Well, what do you think?' and added, 'I rather like the Swiss girl.' Father said, 'I think the other girl is more intelligent and speaks better French.'

Frances wore a little flowered hat for the interview and looked very sweet. She was certainly prettier than the Swiss girl and obviously appealed to Father. She got the job and came to Criccieth for the summer, but frankly, we children thought she was dull, and we certainly never learnt any French from her.

When the holidays ended, Megan went to Allenswood School, but she hadn't been there long before the school closed down and afterwards she went to Garrett Hall School, Banstead. Frances Stevenson, now at loose ends, joined the staff at Downing Street and became my father's secretary. As far as the family was concerned, she was just another employee and we never discussed her. Mother certainly never mentioned her, but she quickly realised what was going on. Probably Megan was the last of the family to become aware of the relationship between Frances and Father, and when it did dawn on her it was a shock, because she liked Frances and had enjoyed her company.

As the years went by, Mother was able to joke about her, which was a very good thing; by then I don't think it hurt her any more. As she got older, Mother began to feel she had done her part to support Father in his political ambitions, and he could go his own way, while she led the life she wanted to lead in Wales. During the whole of their married life, I never heard her run him down in any way, although I think in the end the deep love she had felt for him had just faded away.

In contrast, Father, I am quite certain, loved Mother deeply right to the end of his life. He wanted them both— Mother and Frances.

Frances looked like an English rose, with a lovely complexion. To talk to she seemed meek and mild, but underneath she was as hard as nails. She was possessive and avaricious beyond words, and on many occasions we found that she had carried tales about various members of the family to Father, which upset us all. Amongst ourselves, we always referred to her as 'Flossie'. Father used to call her 'Pussy'.

As her hold over Father increased, she carried the most extraordinary tales about us to my father, and they sometimes came back; poor old A. J. Sylvester—Father's official secretary—used to get the blame. She spread lies about my supposed extravagance when I was first married, and tales about men friends of Megan's. She interfered with personal family filcs which my father kept in his office, and influenced him over money matters.

Even while she was with Father, Frances had other affairs. In the family we never believed that her daughter, Jennifer, was my father's child, because she was so unlike the other members of the family. Jennifer has, I believe, always said that she did not know who her father was. The man concerned was not Father, and proof of that exists. He made a full confession in writing to Father, who told A.J., and A.J. made a full shorthand note of that conversation when it occurred. The statement made to Father was never challenged. I believe this came as a great shock to him, but he loved children, and, presented with Frances's child, treated her as a daughter.

I think Mother was relieved when we were old enough and she could talk to us about Frances. After the war, when Mother returned to Criccieth, she seemed quite content to let Father go his own way, although she was always pleased to see him when he came to North Wales. Mother would never be a doormat, and Father liked to have slaves around him. Although I always disliked Frances I felt sorry for her in some respects, particularly after Father left the House of Commons, because she was nothing more than a slave, and I think she had a dreadful time with him.

While they were in Downing Street, Mother had a considerable influence on the decisions which Father took. He consulted her about everything, and usually took her advice. Father said it was because of Mother's insistence that he gave way to Winston Churchill during the war over the question of building a battleship. Mother thought Winston, then First Lord of the Admiralty, was talking sense, and Father later told him, 'You can have your battleship, but only because my wife says so!'

Throughout the years while Father was in the Government Mother worked tirelessly at Caernarfon to keep his seat for him. At election times he was always travelling up and down the country speaking at meetings for other candidates. She had to represent him in his own constituency, and I believe she worked as hard at electioneering as he ever did. He was grateful, of course, though there were times when she felt she did not get the credit she deserved.

Mother was a calm person, with a firm character and a good sense of humour, without which life would have been very difficult for her. She had had a strict upbringing, and without being sanctimonious in any sense of the word, she had decided ideas on things, including bad language and drink. No one ever used bad language in her presence—or in my father's, for that matter. She didn't drink at all, and when we were older, we children used to go to Father's study in the evening for a drink before dinner, when she would not be there. This was not intended to be underhand, but simply to respect her feelings. Sometimes she would ask us in a good-natured way, 'Did you enjoy your drink?' But she didn't really like to see us drinking.

Father was always moderate in his drinking. I never saw him drinking during the day, and he certainly didn't like champagne. He liked a glass of wine with dinner and towards the end of his life his doctor advised him to have a little Irish whiskey as a night-cap. When we were at home we children, by then grown up, used to enjoy relaxing over a drink in his room and talking to him. He was always a marvellous listener, and these hours were very precious to us.

While Mother's life and behaviour were influenced by the chapel, Father had a much more open-minded approach, but I don't accept suggestions that he was really a pagan at heart.

He believed in God, but he didn't thrust his beliefs down anyone's throat. He used to quote the Bible but he didn't preach about manners and morals. The most important thing in his life was his work, and right from the start he told Mother, 'Maggie, nothing is going to come between me and politics. I am determined to go on and do what I think I should do, come what may.' I am quite certain that right from the beginning Mother knew what kind of a man she had taken on when she agreed to marry him.

Did he have double standards of morality? I suppose in a sense he did, for as we grew up his attitude was rather 'Do as I say, not do as I do'. I remember occasions when he lectured me about my friends and tried to stop me going out when I wanted to. I used to say, 'That's nice, coming from you.' He was concerned about me and Megan, and always wanted to know where we were going, who we were with and when we would be home. I often thought he was over-protective, but realise now that he loved us and wanted to ensure that we came to no harm.

Although he was unfair to Mother in many ways, I have never agreed with people who have tried to sympathise with her position by saying she had a terrible life with him. She didn't. While she was undoubtedly unhappy at times, on the whole she had a very good life, doing what she wanted to do and enjoying it. I have often thought that she was also unfair to Father by refusing some of his requests, particularly dressing up for him. He enjoyed seeing her looking well-dressed, and loved to show her off to his friends. He had good taste and bought her hats, blouses and many other things, which she would not wear. He was generous and expansive, and inclined to be extravagant. He loved entertaining and was a very good host, but Mother, particularly in the early days when we weren't very well off, was thrifty and terrified of over-spending.

Father loved a big welcoming fire, and I really rather agree with him, but Mother would never have one. Sometimes, when Father was expected home, I used to say, 'Oh Mummy, do put some more coal on the fire.' She would reply, 'The fire's all right as it is.' Sometimes she let it go down too far and I can see her now, frantically trying to fan it into life with a newspaper before he came in. So there was often a row when he came home because the fire was nearly out.

Mother never cared about clothes. She was the least conceited person I have ever known. Father used to say to her, 'Why don't you wear that blouse I gave you?' I remember how proud he was of her when she was presented at Court. She had a lovely white dress with a long train lined in pale green chiffon, and the people of Caernarfon had embroidered the train with a leek in white and silver. Father was standing in the drawing-room with some friends when Mother was ushered in. She looked beautiful. Her hair had been styled specially for the occasion and her cheeks were pink with excitement. Father was so overwhelmed when he saw her that his face went absolutely crimson. He was so proud of her; it was a shame that there were so many occasions when she wouldn't please him in this way.

Chapter VI

1914-18

WAR

I was 22 when the war began, and I almost immediately became a VAD. To start with I did some work in the emergency hospital which was set up in the old mansion house on the Wern estate between Criccieth and Porthmadog. Many of the local girls used to go there to help, and although the war seemed a long way away we all thought we were helping. The house at Criccieth where my grandparents had lived and which Mother still owned was empty, so it was let to three Belgian refugee families. One of the refugees, a man named De Vynck, was a gifted wood-carver, and made some beautiful things, some of which can still be found in the Criccieth area. Among them is a portrait in relief of Father, which hangs in Criccieth Memorial Hall.

When Mother started the Welsh Troops Comforts Fund from Number 11 Downing Street, I went to London to help. She had a very good committee, and all over Wales women were knitting scarves, socks and balaclava helmets, and raising money to send chocolate, cigarettes and other comforts to the Welsh troops. Parcels arrived by the score daily, and soon one room at Number 11 became stacked with them; the contents were to be sorted out and re-packed in parcels of identical size and shape before being sent on to the men. They were dispatched to France once a week.

Father had an absolute mania for parcels. When he saw one he immediately wanted to get his hands on it and open it. The sight of so many hundreds of parcels coming into Number 11 dazzled him, and although he knew very well

Selling flags for the Welsh Troops Fund on St. David's Day, 1915. I am pictured with Sir Maurice Hankey.

what they contained he couldn't resist opening one. Mother caught him red-handed, surrounded by paper, string and a pile of khaki socks just as she came down to breakfast, and she was absolutely furious with him. He looked quite shame-faced as she told him off like a naughty little boy.

After my year in France, I could speak the language quite well, and I was much in demand by Father to talk to the French diplomats and Army personnel who began to appear. I used to join them for lunch or dinner, acting as an interpreter. This was not always easy, for the French used by the Army people seemed to be quite different from the French I had learnt. I remember on one occasion struggling desperately to translate 'barbed wire entanglement', when M. Thomas, the French Minister of Munitions, was there to lunch. When Lord Reading, who was also present, made signs of helping me out, Father said, 'No, come on Olwen! You ought to know. You're supposed to be able to speak French!'

I failed completely and protested that that phrase had not appeared in our curriculum, and M. Thomas was most sympathetic. Finally, I was rescued by Lord Reading. Then, as so often on these occasions, I was the only woman present.

There were other times when Father thought I did quite well, and said so. He wrote to me on 8 October 1914, from the Treasury Chambers:

My dearest Llwydyn,

I was delighted to hear of your linguistic triumph on Saturday. Well done, Llwyd bach.

Your letter was most interesting. Mamie is at Walton. I am going to a theatre tonight with Mr. Donald of the *Chronicle*.

Newyddion reit dda o Ffrainc ond drwg o Antwerp. [Quite good news from France, but bad from Antwerp.]

Love Tada.

Father, with Megan, who was selling flags for the French appeal in 1914

Three Welshmen at Number 11 Downing Street, 1915. Left to right, Sir Henry Jones, Lloyd George and the Rev. John Williams, of Brynsiencyn.

It soon became obvious to us all that the war was not going the way it should, and Father became increasingly concerned. He went to France surrounded by great secrecy to see for himself, and he talked to hundreds of soldiers. He was devastated by the slaughter of all the brave young men who were going out to France to be killed within a few weeks. He was appalled by the tactics of General Haig, who was still sending out horses when Father knew that times had changed and that this would be a mechanised war.

The terrible thing was that the Army was trying to fight a war not only with totally inadequate weapons but also without sufficient ammunition for the pathetic guns they did have. As Minister of Munitions, Father managed to harness industry in Britain to produce more weapons and ammunition, and gradually the flow of arms to the Front increased.

As usual, Father made many enemies, but his friendship with Winston Churchill endured, and Winston was often at Number 11. Father was never one to consider other people's convenience, so I suppose it was completely in character when he decided to bring Churchill home for dinner one Sunday evening when Mother was at Walton Heath and everybody else, including the kitchen staff, was either out or away, apart from one. It was the custom in those days for all the members of staff except one to have Sunday evening off, in order that they could attend their various Welsh chapels. The one on duty on that occasion was the 'tweeny', who couldn't have been more than fifteen. The girl, Blodwen, was a niece of Lallie's, and had come to us a short time before from her home near Caernarfon. The doorbell went, and when she answered it she found it was Father's Secretary, who asked, 'Would you be able to make dinner for Mr Lloyd George and Mr Churchill?' Blodwen knew there was a leg of lamb in the larder, but she hesitated. What would her aunt say if she cooked it? The Secretary's insistence that they must have dinner won the day, and Blodwen cooked the

Father with Field Marshal Douglas Haig and Marshal Joffre, during the early part of the 1914-18 war.

Father's visit to France and the trenches during the 1914-18 war.

Father and Winston Churchill, pictured leaving the War Office in 1914.

lamb and made a very nice dinner. She told me the story later, because it was an occasion she never forgot.

After the meal, she got a message asking her to go upstairs. She thought she was going to be reprimanded for something, but both men thanked her very much for the meal, and praised it. But even that didn't prevent her from worrying about what Lallie was going to say when she returned.

In those wartime days, when food was scarce, you didn't cook a whole leg of lamb lightly, and she was terrified at the thought of having to explain where the week's meat supply had gone. Apparently Lallie had warned her when she first came to London: 'If you don't behave yourself, you go straight back to your mother!'

My brother Richard, who had gone to Cambridge and had become a civil engineer, joined the Royal Welch Fusiliers and went to France, where he later caught trench fever and had an awful time.

Father with Dick at Llanystumdwy during the 1914-18 war.

In 1915 I was allowed to go to France as a VAD with Dorothy Hudson, the daughter of Sir Robert Hudson, head of the British Red Cross Society. We were a little under age, but we were keen to go. Sir Robert saw Mother and told her he thought he could arrange it. I didn't see very much of France because I was stuck at Boulogne, where part of the platform at the railway terminus was roped off as a reception area for the hospital trains. I was what they called a cooklet, and I also used to scrub the platform. I used to say to my friends, 'If you see a patch which is cleaner than all the rest, that's my bit.' I worked so hard on it that I really believe you could have eaten off the floor!

We stayed in a chalet, and my bedroom verlooked the railway. I used to hear the troops as they landed from England, and as the trains went out towards the Front the men hung out of the windows and sang.

It was such a contrast to the trains which brought the men back from the trenches. They were packed with wounded, half of them 'sitting cases' who were so bad that they should have been in hospital trains. They were brought from the train to us so that they could receive some medical attention, have their wounds dressed, and so on, before going on to one of the many hospitals along the French coast.

After a while I left Boulogne and was sent about twenty miles inland to a railway junction, where we had a hut in the fields beside the railway. We provided the men with coffee and cocoa as the trains came through. The gratitude of the men was immense. Some of them were in a most pathetic state, and those who needed attention were taken off the train to have their bandages changed. There seemed to be thousands of them passing through every day.

We took our job as VADs very seriously, and worked hard. There wasn't much social life, and most of the time when we went off duty we were so tired that we just went to bed and slept. For the first time I found myself able to go out with friends without parental restrictions, and young officers I

This photograph of Father, Mother and Megan, taken during the early part of the 1914-18 war, when Father was Minister of Munitions, was sold in aid of the National Fund for Welsh Troops.

knew who were passing through would take me out for a few hours. We almost forgot the war as we talked about home and our friends. I knew some very nice young men who escorted me for an evening and afterwards took me back to the villa where I was staying. Our escorts were never allowed in, so we had to say goodnight at the door.

Many of them were killed while they were still little more than boys. One of them was a young man in the Welsh Guards of whom I was very fond. Lady Mond had a party and we went to it together, I wearing Welsh costume with buckled shoes, trimmed with diamanté. During the evening, one of the diamanté buckles came off and my friend put it into his pocket. We forgot all about it, but I never saw him again after that night. He was only about nineteen or twenty when he was killed.

I was in France for about a year. It was decided that I should return home when my younger brother, Gwilym, was sent out to France, mainly because Mother was becoming so worried and unhappy with two sons fighting in the war. So back I went to London and Number 11, and continued working for the Red Cross there. I also helped at a canteen for the troops. Mother had flung herself into the war effort, and was working very hard to provide comforts for the men.

One day Mother told me that a young Army captain, whose family she knew in Wales, was coming to tea with his sister. Their father was a doctor at Blaenau Ffestiniog, and although our families knew each other well I had never met Tom Carey Evans before. It was love at first sight for both of us. I loved his voice, and I thought he was the nicest young man I had ever met. The thought came to me instantly: I would like to marry that man. Apparently I clicked with him, too. He asked me to go to the theatre next day with him and his sister, which I did, and the evening was a great success.

It was Easter, 1916, and I went to Criccieth. Tom, who was on leave after returning from Gallipoli, went to Ffestiniog to stay with his people, and for the next two or three weeks we saw each other every day. Tom was waiting for his orders, and when they came he said to me, 'You know what I want, don't you? I would like you to marry me.' I didn't say yes—then. Although I knew I loved him, I didn't fancy the idea of being engaged to a myth who wasn't there. He had been posted to Mesopotamia, and goodness knows when we would meet again, if ever. The parting was awful, but he had a birthday in June, and by that time I was quite definite about what I wanted to do—and I knew I would be very happy. I cabled him in Mesopotamia: 'Happy Birthday. Yes. Love Olwen.'

Father and Mother knew quickly after that first meeting that there was something between us, but they did not try to influence me in any way. I thought Father was very funny— he kept going to the window when Tom was due to arrive, and looked at him in an odd way when he came to lunch. They were both very pleased when we told them we were getting married. Father was always very fussy about our friends and with whom we went out, but Tom fitted in very well with the family. Apart from anything else, he was a Welshman, and I had always felt I could never marry anyone except a Welshman.

During the school holidays I had the job of looking after Megan, who was then thirteen. She couldn't understand why Tom and I wanted to go out alone, and thought she ought to be asked to come. So to start with she didn't at all like this young man who had come between us even though we relented once or twice and took her with us.

Tom was eight years older than I, and had joined the Indian Medical Service a few years before the war. When we met he had just gone through the horrors of Gallipoli, where he won the Military Cross and was three times mentioned in despatches, and following his leave he was sent to Mesopot-

amia. Later he was appointed to organise medical relief for
the civilian population in Bagdad, and he became the
surgeon in charge of the civil hospital there, which was run
by nuns. A very high proportion of people in the Middle
East at that time suffered from kidney stones and urinary
complaints, and the experience he gained there made him a
specialist in this field. While he was there, he wrote me some
very interesting and amusing letters, telling me of incidents
at the hospital.

One of his patients, a very important lady from some
distance away, arrived one day for an operation, accompanied by a bodyguard of eight warriors, armed to the teeth.
They were told they couldn't go into the operating theatre,
but they insisted, and, rather persuaded by the sight of the
spears, Tom told the sister-in-charge to let them in. The
operation began, and at the sight of blood first one and then
another of the warriors slipped to the ground in dead faints.
Eventually every one of them had gone down, and one by
one they were carried outside to recover while the operation
continued without interruption.

Another of his stories which greatly amused me concerned
another of his patients, a rich Arab. Tom left him well
wrapped up in bed, with hot water bottles all round him, and
strict instructions that he must not be given anything to
drink, not even water. Some time later, the nurse assigned to
his care went rushing out to find the Mother Superior who
was in charge. 'Ma Mère, ma Mère, come quickly!' she
shrieked. 'He's drinking his hot water bottles!' Being surrounded by bottles of water was too much for the patient, who
was emptying first one and then another down his parched
throat!

Tom was very generous and was always sending me
presents by whatever means he could, usually by someone
who happened to be coming home. One of his first presents
to me was a beautiful pendant from Port Said, and he also
sent Persian rugs. Over the year I acquired so many Persian

rugs that more recently I've been able to supply the whole family with them.

After my telegram promising to be his wife, he arranged with his sister to buy an engagement ring on his behalf. She went to Carrington's, the London jewellers, and at his behest brought away four rings so that I could make my choice. I didn't realise until long afterwards that the one I chose was the most expensive.

The conduct of the war, and the very strong feeling that we might lose it, continued to worry Father and his Cabinet colleagues, but it was with a great deal of reluctance that he finally agreed to step in as Prime Minister. He valued his friendship with Mr. Asquith, and greatly disliked the idea of putting him aside. It had, however, become apparent to everyone close to him that Asquith was no longer able to continue as the first statesman. There were many stories about his disinterest and lack of direction in Cabinet meetings, and there were those who criticised him openly for resorting too much to the whisky bottle. I remember being reprimanded by Mother one day for passing some casual remark about Asquith 'not knowing what was going on, because he had drunk too much and had fallen asleep.' Mother was quite sharp as she reminded me that things seen and heard about my Father's Cabinet colleagues were not to be repeated— ever! By December, 1916, the point of no return had been reached. The country had a new Prime Minister, and we moved into Number 10.

The organisation at Number 10 was quite different then from what it is now. Whereas nowadays there is a flat at the top of the building for the use of the Prime Minister, and outside contractors are called in when any large-scale catering has to be done, at that time we occupied the whole house, and it fell upon Mother and Lallie to organise the catering. Moving was a simple matter—we walked in from next door, by the garden gate. I loved living at Number 10, for there

The War Cabinet at Number 10, 1916.

was always something going on. Famous people came and went, and Number 10 seemed to be the hub of the universe.

Just before lunch one day, General Smuts came and told Mother, 'Your husband has sent me to tell you they are coming up, and there will be three of us.' He added, 'Why are Monday mornings always so terribly sad? We seem to get all the bad news on Mondays.' The latest push in France had been followed by thousands of unnecessary casualties, and the General was looking very downcast. Then there was a noise and Father arrived in a great rush, as he always did. General Smuts smiled. 'We can't be depressed for long with this man around!' he said.

Sir Edward Carson was with Father, and the three of them, with Mother and myself, sat down to lunch. This kind of thing used to happen almost every day, and we felt we were involved with the war and everything that was going on.

The war and winning it were uppermost in Father's thoughts at that time. One of his Cabinet colleagues said to him once, 'Lloyd George, you have war on the brain!' He replied, 'Yes, I have. I can think of nothing else but our boys out there, lacking ammunition and weapons. I only wish you had it more on the brain!'

Before the war, when he dealt with strikes, he used to go and talk to the men who were involved, and now he did not rely on reports from the generals. He talked to the captains and the majors, and found out for himself what life was like for the men in the trenches. Father was always a very good listener, and I have heard it said that he often sat quietly in Cabinet meetings, just listening.

Even with the problems of the war to contend with, Father still found time to write letters, and not only to members of the family. He wrote to friends and sons of friends who were away fighting, and one such letter evidently went to Wedg-wood Benn, later Lord Stansgate and father of Tony Wedg-wood Benn. The letter was obviously greatly appreciated, for I found a reply from him among Mother's things.

Benn wrote to Mother: 'It is wonderfully kind of him with the whole world on his shoulders to find time to think even of writing. I have sent the letter for my mother to see—she will be proud.

'I am being so bold as to ask you to thank the Prime Minister—in order to make quite sure that he knows how much I appreciate his kindness.'

One morning Mother told me that something particularly interesting was happening. Father was going with General Du Cane to Wormwood Scrubs to see a new machine. It was all quite secret, for the new machine was the first British tank which was to be tried out in the prison grounds. The tank changed the course of the war completely, and Father was delighted to be able to send tanks into battle instead of horses, which no longer had any place in war.

The whole family felt a deep sadness when dear Uncle Lloyd died in the Spring of 1917 at the age of 76. He had been failing for some time, and I believe he died a happy man, for he had lived long enough for Father to achieve the goal of Prime Minister which Uncle Lloyd had always felt was his. There was no doubt that once Father went into Number 10, Uncle Lloyd believed that everything would soon be all right, for he had supreme faith in Father's ability.

With the death of Uncle Lloyd, I felt I had lost a very dear friend. Criccieth without him was never quite the same, and when I returned there I felt for a long time quite lonely without him to talk to. Over the years we had corresponded regularly, exchanging all the family news. Only one of his letters now remains in my possession, one which he wrote on 31 March 1911, for my birthday. He wrote, often underlining to emphasise his words:

Uncle Lloyd is not one for *dates* at all, as you all well know. But when he comes to realise his dear one's *birth date,* it touches him to the bottom of his heart, with great joy, and sincerest prayers for their true happiness—with very many returns.

Too late to get any chance to send you some *little token* of our greetings and good wishes, but Uncle Lloyd will certainly remember it again when convenient, Llwyd bach.

Very glad to get your letters always, highly pleased to observe the great progress you are making in all respects, in taking good care to turn your great advantages with your education in that renowned place, and by doing so preparing yourself for your future life of service and true happiness. Splendid letter your last—like all we have the pleasure of receiving so regular from you, Llwyd bach.

There is a brief reference to Father:

Got word today from London—there attending to his great work with his Insurance Scheme, and he tells me that he is completely restored.

The letter ends:

Gwilym is to come next week I guess, and Llwydyn's turn will come soon, too. We are all well. Best wishes, my dearest Llwyd. Uncle Lloyd.

I didn't see Tom again for over a year, but we decided that as soon as he got leave we would be married. My worst fears were almost realised when the ship bringing him home was torpedoed. By the greatest of good fortune he escaped without serious injury, but he lost most of his possessions and arrived home with just the uniform he was wearing, a rather shabby one. Father knew the ship had been torpedoed, and there were some anxious days until it was known that Tom was safe. He kept the news of the torpedoeing from me, but I began to worry when Tom did not arrive when I expected him.

Just when I was beginning to get frantic, a telegram arrived telling me that Tom was safe. Lord Carson, who was at the Admiralty at the time, happened to be lunching at Number 10 and he was able to interpret the telegram for me as it was worded in official language. He told me that Tom's ship had been mined, but he was all right and would be home in a few days. Eventually Tom arrived, just four days before the wedding.

Many people thought that, as the Prime Minister's daughter, I should be married at St. Margaret's, Westminster, the church where all the big society weddings took place. Father was completely against this. Tom and I wanted a Welsh wedding, and since we had to be married in London because of Father's Cabinet duties, and not in our beloved Wales, we decided that the wedding should be on 19 June at the Welsh Baptist Chapel in Castle Street, London. This was the chapel which Father and other members of the household attended, and since both Tom and myself were Baptists it seemed a suitable choice.

Because of the war, it was to be a quiet wedding, with an informal reception at home just for members of the family and very close friends. Father took a couple of hours off to give me away. There was a Cabinet meeting that morning, and apparently he looked at his watch and told his colleagues, 'I'm sorry, but we will have to end the meeting here. I have an important engagement this afternoon.'

The family sat down to lunch, but I was much too nervous to eat anything. As the only fair-haired member of the family, I always appeared to be paler than the rest of them, but on this occasion I was deathly white—just like a lily, one of the maids said. I drove to the church with Father in his Rolls-Royce, and I can't recall what we said on the way. I don't believe he offered me any advice at all, but if he did, it certainly didn't sink in.

When we first got engaged, Father had asked me, 'Are you quite sure you love him? Would you be frightfully upset if he

Tom and myself, the day before our wedding, 1917.

didn't come home?' I said yes, I would be, and he seemed to be satisfied. If he didn't give me any advice before my wedding, he certainly didn't make any financial arrangements, either. Afterwards he sent me cheques, sometimes very generous ones, and he paid the school fees at Roedean for my two daughters, but I never had a regular allowance from him, as most girls in my position expected to have at that time.

Neither did I get any pre-marital advice from Mother. The facts of life were totally ignored by both my parents, and in those days there wasn't much sex education at school either. Years afterwards, when I was talking to Mother about this, she said, 'Oh, well, you were marrying a doctor, so I thought it was all right.'

Once the date of the wedding was fixed, the presents started to arrive. A cheque came from Mr Bonar Law, who had taken over from Father as Chancellor of the Exchequer, with a friendly little note: 'I asked my sister to get a present for you and she told me that she was sure you would prefer to buy it yourself, so that you would get something which you would like to have, and that seemed to me reasonable.

'I am sure you have forgiven me for bursting in when you were "engaged" the other day, and I can give you both a certificate of good behaviour. Again, wishing you every happiness.'

The wedding was timed for 2.30 p.m. Apart from the address, which was in English, the ceremony was almost entirely in Welsh, and included Welsh hymns and musical arrangements.

Father received a telegram from the King, congratulating us all, and there were even some celebrations at Criccieth, where a cannon was fired. The Chairman of the local council sent a telegram which read: 'Criccieth sends affectionate greetings and best wishes.'

We had planned a simple wedding, cutting out as many of the trimmings as we could. I wore white, and even though

From my wedding album, 1917.

my dress was far less elaborate than it probably would have been in normal times, I thought it was quite beautiful. It was made of satin, and the train was in chiffon, lined in shell pink. My sister, Megan, and one of Tom's cousins, Gwendoline Armstrong Jones, were the bridesmaids, and both had pretty, short dresses. Tom and his brother, Gwilym, who was a lieutenant in the Royal Welch Fusiliers, both wore uniform.

A group of wounded soldiers from Millbank Hospital in London formed a guard of honour as we left the church, and next day Mother invited them to tea at Number 10 to thank them. I was very touched to find there were also some girl munition workers waiting at the church door to present me with a beautiful bouquet of carnations.

Even though the reception was quite informal, we couldn't get married without the traditional multi-tiered wedding cake. Quite a few eyebrows were raised when the guests saw it in all its splendour, dominating the tea table. How had the Prime Minister managed to get all that sugar for the icing? For sugar and a lot of other things were rationed, or difficult to come by. One of my friends, who had been married just a few weeks before, said to me, 'What it is to be the daughter of the Prime Minister, and have icing on your wedding cake!' I told her to go and try some—for all that beautiful icing was a sham, carefully modelled out of white card!

Almost immediately after the wedding, Tom and I left for Waterloo Station on our way to Tintagel, in Cornwall, where we spent our honeymoon. We thought we would be lucky if we had a week together, but Tom's recall did not come as quickly as we thought, and we were able to go on to Cardiff to spend a few days with friends, and then on to Criccieth before the telegram arrived.

I returned to Number 10, and the pain of separation after such a short time together was eased a little when I found that I was expecting a baby. One night, before my daughter was born, I was alone at Number 10 with Father when we heard the most awful bang. We met on the landing as Father came from his bedroom and I from mine, and heard a second bang. We went to the front door, and found the police outside.

It was the first Zeppelin raid on London, and we stood in the middle of the road like a couple of children looking up into the sky to see what was happening. We thought the bombs had dropped on the House of Commons and on Buckingham Palace, but one fell near Swann and Edgar's in Piccadilly and the other somewhere near Camberwell. One of the policemen looked at Father and said, 'Don't you think you ought to go in, Sir?' We realised the sense of that, and both went inside and back to bed. Next day, Father said to me, 'Llwydyn, I don't want you to be up here with these raids,' and I was sent to Wales.

News reached me regularly from London in letters, usually from Mother but sometimes from Father, too. At the end of 1917, both had been unwell, and on 9 December Mother wrote:

> I am up today, and so is Tada, and gone to Walton. He was in bed Thursday and yesterday. Today he got up for breakfast and had two or three men to breakfast—from one extreme to the other. He ought to have had his breakfast in bed, and it is really no use being in bed like he is, and then having an audience all day.

Part of the letter was missing, but Mother added:

> He has had the bismuth tabloids you had. Of course I had to pretend to Dr. Warner [the doctor] that I was sending them to you. He was afraid he would want to see him.

There was another letter next day. Mother wrote:

> I am better today but must keep indoors until chest clears. Tada is better but feeling rather cheap. Lord Reading here

to lunch, also Gen. Smuts and Lord Wilbur. Tada has just gone off now to Manpower Committee.

After some gossip, the letter goes on:

Poor old Wil [Gwilym] is in hospital with something like pyresia or pyretia—what is it? Something to do with the throat. I have hunted for that dictionary you studied for hours one night. Can't find it. Tada was upset, it seems, at Walton last night. I knew nothing of it here. Wire this morning as follows: "Condition Major G. Ll. G. slight pyresia. Progress very satisfactory." He is at No. 14 General Boulogne. Write him, will you? Anyway he is safe from the Huns there. I hope it won't interfere with his leave.

Across the top of the letter she had scribbled as an after-thought: 'Such a nice present for you from Dundee from Capt. Gownet or Gowmour, IMS—after dinner coffee set.'

A further letter was dated the day after, 11 December, in reply to one from me. Mother wrote:

I had your letter. I am so glad you are having such glorious sunshine there. It has been quite fine here today, but it rained in torrents Sunday, and yesterday *snow* at Walton, of course.

Megan wrote me three sheets from Walton on Sunday, poor mite. She has had a fiver for Christmas present from Lord Colwyn.

I am much better today, only I am keeping indoors for two or three days until cough goes. Tada seems himself again today. Dr. Addison here to lunch so we had a nice time. Who called just now but old Col. Fryer. I really could not be bothered with him so I sent word to say I was not well, nice excuse when you don't want to see people.

The raid was the night before I was bad. Wasn't I lucky? Tada had gone to Walton, and at three in the morning old Wilkam minus teeth came to call me. Got up, went down.

At 3.30 they said all clear. Back to bed, called again at
four. Then they came with a vengeance, dropped a bomb
in the grass by H. of Commons, one in St. James Park, in
front of Sir George Riddle's house, exploded. Two behind
where Lizzie lives. I forget where the other one dropped.
They dropped six or seven very near us.

Next night Tada was ill and I never slept a wink. My
throat burnt like fire so I might as well be in the basement
had there been a raid. I had two sleepless nights running.
We were up from three to six, and then went back to bed
before the all clear that came at 6.45. They had four down
here and two collided in Belgium.

Isn't it splendid about Jerusalem? Lady Lewis writes to
say that Tom has been splendid about Arthur's grave.
Fond love, Mam.

In another letter about the same time, dated simply
'Sunday evening', she wrote:

Tada brought Megan up to go to hear the Messiah at the
Foundlings Hospital. It was very good—the Huddersfield
Choir, Dilys Jones, contralto, and Agnes Nicholson, sop.,
Robert Radford.

Dick has turned up and looks well. I hope Roberta did
not excite herself and tire herself going to Chester to meet
him. Poor old Wil. Dick was four hours in Boulogne not
knowing Wil was there. I hope if Wil is there he can see
him on his way back, but Wil hopes to be away in a week
then he gets three weeks sick leave. That will be nice.

I suppose you are having Betty up to Bryn to sleep with
you tomorrow when new maid arrives. She will like to
come. We cannot come before Friday as the draw at Sel-
fridges is not until Thursday.

I was at St. Dunstan's. Saw Sister Pat. She is a dear and
wishes to be remembered to you. She had a p.c. of Tada in
her den. She wanted me to tell you it was next best thing
to having you.

Only one of Father's letters remains. He wrote on 10 Downing Street notepaper on 20 March 1918:

My dear Llwydyn.

Thanks for your jolly letter. I am now down in the House of Commons ready for Questions. Shipbuilding. The sky is clear and looks as if an air raid might scatter our enemies soon!

Love and luck to you, Taid.

The letter ends in Welsh: 'Sut mae Nain? [How is Grandma?]

He was thrilled that I was to have a baby, and even more overjoyed when my daughter was born on 25 April. Mother was with me at Brynawelon, and Father wrote on 25 April from Number 10:

To all my sweethearts at Brynawelon—great and small. Good luck to the dear little recruit that has arrived to reinforce the Brynawelon garrison. Sarah woke me up at 3 a.m. with the good news. I was delighted and especially delighted that Olwen has started her family with a little girl. She can reserve the boys for Granny—Grandpa prefers the little girls. Wel done Llwydyn bach. Fondest love from old Grandpa.

Mother wrote back to him next day:

My dearest old Taid.

So you are pleased with your little grand-daughter. I knew you would be. You were full of the Brynawelon front this morning and nothing about the war. Olwen is getting on nicely, and the little girl is the most quaint little thing you ever saw. She is so matter of fact and old-fashioned. I'll take all the boys willingly, but I know how silly you will be with the two little girlies.

Fondest love.

Your ever loving Margaret.

There was never any doubt in my mind over names for my new daughter. I told Mother, 'She is going to be called

Margaret Lloyd, after you.' When I and my brothers and sisters were born there was nothing simple about naming us. Father took a deep personal interest in every one of our names, and consulted the Mabinogion, the book of traditional Welsh legends, before he was satisfied that the names he had chosen for us were right.

I was only too pleased that he finally settled on Olwen for me, because Mother told me I was very nearly called Bronwen, which I would not have liked. My English friends found Olwen difficult enough to say, and at school I was always called 'Georgie'.

We knew very well that Father would want to have a hand in naming my daughter, and Mother said, 'There'll be another letter from your father tomorrow, with all sorts of suggestions for names.' Sure enough, the letter came. He wrote: 'Don't you think it would be nice if the baby were called Fioled [Violet]?' I can see Mother's face now as she chuckled over the letter. 'Well, too late, old boy', she said. 'She's called Margaret.' She had taken the precaution of registering Margaret before Father could interfere. She had a great sense of humour and was really funny at times, as well as showing foresight.

Mother went back to London but I stayed on at Criccieth for a time with Margaret. Seven months later, in November, when I was back at Criccieth again, Mother telephoned me to say that the war was over.

She said, 'We have just been into your bedroom [which overlooked Downing Street], and Father leant out of the window to wave to the crowds. It's been a wonderful evening.'

The excitement and thankfulness that the bloodiest of all wars had finally ended was felt by us all, and our greatest wish now was to see our menfolk home again. Margaret was almost eighteen months old when her father saw her for the first time.

Chapter VII

1919-22

INDIA

The war had ended, and for those of us with husbands and sons on active service the first sensations were those of relief that the shooting had stopped. We all looked forward to the day when our loved ones would come home, but for many of us there was still a long time to wait. The war had been over for almost a year before I saw Tom again. It was an odd sensation to have been married to someone for over two years and to have spent so little time in his company. Although I had known of him for almost the whole of my life, we had spent only a few weeks together—during our brief courtship, and then the three weeks or so after our marriage before he went back to the Middle East. When people asked me, 'Does your husband like shooting?' or some other activity, I had to say I didn't really know, and I realised how little I knew about him. Tom, for his part, was cherishing a mental picture of our daughter, Margaret, as a baby of a few months old, and when eventually he did return and we stood together looking at her asleep in her cot, he seemed quite shocked.

'She's very large,' he exclaimed, and I felt as though I had produced a monster! After all, he was a doctor, and knew all about babies. Next morning, however, when Margaret ran into our bedroom, he could see she was a perfectly normal toddler, exactly the size you would expect a child of nearly eighteen months to be!

While we waited for Tom to return, life at Number 10 went on. Father had to spend a great deal of time in Paris, working out the Peace Treaty, and we often went over to spend a few days with him in the beautiful flat in the Champs Elysées which had been put at his disposal. He decided at the outset that since he was going to spend a great deal of time in the French capital, he would be much more comfortable in his own apartment, with his own people around him, than he would be in a hotel.

When he was free, usually at weekends, he took us out for the day to see the sights of Paris. We got a warm welcome wherever we went—hotels, cafés and theatres. One hotel was renamed after Megan. Not all our visits with Father were pleasant, for one day he took us to the scene of the battlefield near Verdun, where soldiers had been buried up to their shoulders and died with their bayonets in their hands. Buildings were still spattered with blood and bore lasting blemishes where bullets had ricochetted and cannons had blasted their way through solid stone. It had been the war to end all wars, and at that time we all believed it could never happen again.

Apart from Paris, there was great activity at home, for the end of the war was followed almost immediately by a General Election. Since Father was busy elsewhere, it fell upon Mother to fight for his seat in his place. I think it was this election which really proved her worth, and showed the people of Wales and beyond that she was a forcible character in her own right. With characteristic energy, she toured the countryside speaking at meetings, and in her hands his Caernarfon seat was safe.

Father's popularity, both in the House of Commons and outside, was never higher than it was at this time, and on 16 April 1919, he made a speech in the House which moved Austen Chamberlain to write to Mother:

> May an old opponent and present colleague of your husband be permitted to offer you his hearty congratulations on the Prime Minister's speech this afternoon?
>
> I believe that I express the universal opinion in the House—at any rate I heard this on all sides and I heard no

other view—when I say that for power of expression, for moderation and therefore, impressiveness, for masterly arrangement and for courage, he never did anything better if he ever did as well.

He spoke as a statesman with the breadth of view and the gravity befitting his high position and immense responsibilities. We were all grateful to him and in such a mood we are all glad to give him any help we can.

My wife tells me that she was on the point of saying to you something of this kind in the Gallery when someone else came up to speak to you and she was prevented. She wishes me therefore to join her in my expressions of admiration for this great speech which was as great speeches are—more than a speech, an act.'

The Treaty of Versailles was signed in the summer of 1919, very shortly after Tom came home, and when Father returned from Paris, Mother, Tom and myself all went to Victoria Station to meet him. The red carpet was down, and we found that the King was also going to the station to welcome Father home. It was an unforgettable occasion for us all, and I learnt afterwards that it was the first time the King had been to meet one of his ministers.

Instead of getting into the car with us, as he had originally intended, Father was invited to ride in the Royal car with the King and accompany him back to Buckingham Palace. Tom and I followed with Mother, who was escorted into the Palace, while we sat in the car in the courtyard, waiting for them. Then, a footman came and asked us, too, to go inside. Tom was horrified and said he wasn't dressed for the occasion, because he was wearing a well-worn old Army uniform and felt he was much too shabby to meet the King and Queen. I told him it was a Royal command and must be obeyed, so into the Palace we went.

The King and Queen were standing in one of the reception rooms at the top of a very grand flight of stairs, which seemed never-ending to us as we walked slowly up to be

greeted in a very friendly way when we were presented. The
Prince of Wales and young Princess Mary were also there,
and we talked with them all for about half-an-hour. The
Queen was most surprised to hear that I had an eighteen-
month-old daughter whom her father had not seen until he
came home, and that we had been parted for so long. 'But
your father is Prime Minister,' the Queen said, in amaze-
ment. 'Why ever didn't he bring your husband home?'

I could say with complete honesty that such a thing had
never occurred to any of us. We never at any time thought
such preferential treatment was attached to the Prime
Minister's household.

I thought Princess Mary was really beautiful, and a sweet,
shy girl, so full of hope and expectation for the future.

Father and mother had a very cordial relationship with the
King and Queen, and on several occasions were invited to
stay at Balmoral and other Royal residences. Sometimes the
Queen sent small presents back with Father or Mother for
myself and Megan, and I still have a silver-topped salt cellar
which the Queen sent.

Because Tom was in the Indian Medical Service, I knew
from the outset that I would be following him to India.
When his posting eventually came, it was as Residency
Medical Officer to the State of Mysore, and so it was in
Bangalore that we set up our first home together.

I waited impatiently with the other Service wives until a
ship was available. I had to make the desperately hard
decision to leave my daughter, Margaret, behind, because of
the uncertainty of what lay ahead for Tom and me in the
immediate future. Luckily, she could stay with Mother and
Father in Downing Street, making frequent visits to
Criccieth, so I was not worried about the care she would
have. She had a playmate of her own age, too, in my brother
Richard's daughter, Valerie, who spent long periods with
Mother.

At last I was given a passage to India on the SS Patricia, from Liverpool. I set out eagerly, looking forward to the three weeks' voyage and the new life which lay ahead. I wasn't at all prepared for the discomforts which we would have to endure, nor did I suspect that the three weeks would be six before we eventually arrived. SS Patricia had been in service as a troopship, and was distinctly the worse for wear. In normal circumstances, the ship would have had a refit before sailing again, but at that time there was such a shortage of ships that every one which would float was pressed into service.

To say the ship was overcrowded was an understatement. She was carrying twice her usual complement, mostly Service officers and young wives, and the congestion was unbelievable. Four people occupied cabins for two, and from some berths you could lie in bed and touch the ceiling. There were two sittings for meals, but, worse still, the ship's plumbing could not cope with the numbers, and water had to be used sparingly both for personal washing and laundry.

Before I sailed, Father offered me some good advice. Even though I was married, and a mother, and felt quite worldly-wise, he was worried about my ability to look after myself. We were having lunch at Number 10 at the time, with some of his Cabinet colleagues, and I remember replying, 'You're a fine one to give advice!' Everybody laughed at that, much to Father's discomfiture.

There have been times when being the Prime Minister's daughter had its advantages, and there were some such occasions on this voyage. When we got into the Bay of Biscay, which inevitably lived up to its reputation for rough seas, the ship's radio failed, and we were out of communication with the shore bases. It wasn't until afterwards that I knew there was some consternation at home, and questions were asked in the House of Commons about the ship's seaworthiness. When we reached Marseilles, the crew mutinied. As we waited while essential repairs were carried out and the water system was overhauled, Father wrote to the British Consul with a message for me. He told me to disembark and wait for the next P. and O. vessel to arrive.

Not for the first time, I disobeyed him. What I wanted most was to get to India as quickly as possible, and I refused to consider a further delay while I waited for another ship. So I just ignored the message. We were able to go ashore, so a party of us decided to go to Monte Carlo, where we had two nights in a hotel and I paid my first visit to a casino. I won a modest £6 with my first chip—which was Number Six—and bought a blouse with my winnings. I met some friends from London who were on holiday there, and who were very surprised to see me because they had said goodbye to me when I sailed and thought I was on my way to India! Altogether it was a very pleasant break.

Back on board, we found that several hundred Arabs had embarked for Aden, and the all-pervading smell of ghee, the oil they used for cooking, made us all feel permanently sick. We expected to sail immediately, but there was a further delay, waiting for one of the ship's engineering staff who had gone ashore and failed to return.

Eventually we sailed, but only as far as Malta, where there was a further week's delay for more repairs. Since I had never been to Malta, I thought I would make the most of the time by spending the week on the island. But we were frustrated again, for there was a case of smallpox on board, and while the patient was taken to hospital in Malta, we were all put into quarantine for ten days. So all I saw of Malta was Valetta harbour and the rooftops beyond.

Luckily there was an official on the island who had met Mother, and when he heard that I was among the passengers he came on board to see what he could do to help us. He did some shopping for myself and my friends, and the British Consul sent us crates of oranges and newspapers from home.

Once we were on our way again, we started organising games and entertainment on board. I discovered that one of the deck-hands was Welsh-speaking and came from Criccieth. I chatted to him in Welsh, and he made rope quoits for us for one of our deck games. There was excitement whenever another ship came into view, and particularly for me when one was a ship I had launched during the war. The captain sent me greetings over the radio, which raised my spirits enormously.

At Aden, the Arabs disembarked, and once more I was lucky enough to have friends ashore who asked me to lunch. Eventually we reached Bombay, where Tom was waiting, and we had four happy days there before proceeding to Bangalore. Those four days passed almost in a haze, for with the change of climate, the heat and the trials of the journey, I felt exhausted, and I am ashamed to say that when we were invited to a dinner party with some friends of Tom's, I was so tired I fell asleep. Tom was amused and kept apologising on my behalf, but he never let met forget it.

Then it was time to catch the train for Bangalore, which I found had a reasonably pleasant climate. Most of the people on the station lived in bungalows, but we had a two-storey house, reasonably well-furnished but with no modern plumbing or sanitation. Taking a bath was a most primitive arrangement. The excitement of being in these new surroundings soon wore off when I found that, as a white woman, I was not allowed to do anything at all in the house. I got so bored that in the end I had to do what all the other women were doing—gossiping and socialising. I thought it was a stupid way of life, but there was nothing else to do, and since I didn't believe in half-measures, I threw myself into the life and tried to enjoy it.

India was a country of great contrasts. On the one hand there were the vast riches of the princes, and on the other the appalling poverty of the masses. The maharajahs wielded enormous power, and I thought they were a very mixed lot. Some, like the Maharajah of Mysore, did their best for their people, and Mysore was relatively progressive, with schools for the children, and hospitals. It took me a long time to get used to the way of life which European women were forced to lead in India, which meant doing the same thing at the same time every day. We worked in the house in the morning, which generally meant telling the servants what to do, and doing trivial tasks like arranging flowers, and we rested in the afternoon, when it was often too hot to think of doing anything else.

I felt enormous sympathy with the District Commissioners, who had huge territories to govern and received very little pay. Their children had to be sent home to Britain to be educated, and often they were separated from their wives for long periods. The wives were often bored, because tradition and custom meant there was so little they were allowed to do, beyond playing tennis or joining in club dances and other activities. I felt that many wives lacked understanding of their husbands' work and position, and sadly many marriages went adrift.

Servants were plentiful, and all of us seemed to have a great many. They did all the marketing, the cooking, the housework and the gardening, looked after the children, and did just about everything which had to be done. They did the cooking on stone-built open fires, and often they would congregate to help each other. Most of them were extremely loyal, and the only danger was that they would spoil the children, for they loved youngsters and would do anything for them.

At that time, Indian women were very much third class citizens. In the maharajahs' palaces, they lived in purdah, usually in a separate establishment. Today the state of women in India is very different, and the girls, certainly of the higher castes, are educated so that many follow careers in the professions, including medicine. In the 1920s, the caste system was absolute, and the lowest of them, the millions of untouchables, lived in ghastly conditions. They were not allowed to touch food, they received no education, and they could do only the most menial tasks.

I had the greatest admiration for Gandhi and what he was trying to do for India, and for the poor in particular. I thought he was a very great leader. I never had the opportunity of meeting him myself, but I recall that Father was greatly impressed when he met him at Churt. He told me later that he thought him a most extraordinary man, with an almost mystical presence. Gandhi arrived wearing a white dhoti, the traditional Indian garb with which he was always associated. Knowing in advance that he would refuse food, Father scoured the countryside for fresh goat's milk, not so easy to obtain at that time. Gandhi refused that, too, and would only accept a glass of water.

But the most extraordinary thing about his visit was that during the whole of the time he was there, a little black cat squatted at his feet. The cat did not belong to the household, for Father always had dogs about the place, and didn't particularly like cats. This one turned up as soon as Gandhi arrived, and went when he left. No one knew where it had come from, and it was never seen again.

One big preoccupation for me was writing letters home, and since I had always been a prolific correspondent, this came easily. We couldn't wait for the mail to arrive from England, and I got a steady stream of news from Mother about Margaret's progress, as well as all the other activities in Downing Street and elsewhere. One letter told me, with three exclamation marks, that Megan was being a bridesmaid—for the fifth time. In her case, the old adage 'Three times a bridesmaid, never a bride' turned out to be true, but I don't think anyone thought then that Megan would choose to remain single.

Much as she disliked the social round, Mother enjoyed meeting people, and she and Father were in constant demand as guests at all kinds of functions. Her letters to me were full of descriptions of these, with a many candid comments of her own thrown in! She did a lot of constituency work for Father, opening sales, presiding at meetings and carrying out many of the duties which he was unable to perform because of his commitments at Westminster or abroad. I think she enjoyed doing this for him—and it gave her an excuse to revisit Criccieth. In any case, she never wanted to go too far from home while she had Margaret in her care.

Father took Megan with him whenever he could. They missed Mother when she was away from them, and there was a letter to Mother from Father in the early part of the 1920s which underlines that. Father wrote 'Yn fy ngwely' [in bed] at Walton Heath, to Mother who had apparently then just returned to Number 10 from Criccieth:

Hen gariad. Glad you are coming back, although you think Megan and I don't want you because we are bad correspondents. Beth am Dafydd 'te, 'rhen Fagi! [What about your David then, old Maggi!] Megan and I never received a single word from you from the moment you left Criccieth until we returned, although we wrote several letters.

I have had a bad time. I felt for some time a bad attack coming. I took the sea voyage in the hope of averting it. Bertrand Dawson tells me that if I had gone to St. Remo by train, and returned by train, and filled the interval with the intense hard work I had to put in, I should have had a bad breakdown, and done bad work into the bargain. He tells me I must knock off for a fortnight at least.

I go down on Thursday to Philip Sassoon's near Folkstone. Come down early tomorrow and bring the two Megs. We can motor together to Folkestone on Thursday.

I get up this afternoon for the first time. Hope you have got rid of your head throbs. Mine still worry me.

Father was enormously proud of Mother when she took part in political campaigns on his behalf. He wrote to her on 14 February 1921:

My dearest M.

Accounts pouring in from every quarter are full of your almost unexampled triumphal tour. It looks as if you had saved Ernie. [Ernest Evans, MP for Cardiganshire.] He and his agents think so.

Then, underscored in heavy black ink, the letter goes on:

Write me what your impressions are as to the prospects . . . I enclose a few notes for your further speeches. Fond love. Cinio mawr swyddogol heno [big official dinner tonight]. I wish you to Cardigan.

Megan also wrote to Mother in characteristic style, with afterthoughts written all over the top of the first page.

Darling Mams,

We are all thrilled at the daily reports we receive of your doings in Cardigan. Tada is highly delighted. He spent the weekend at Chequers, where Byng[one of the dogs] unfortunately bit little Wil [William George's son] in the heel. He is alright now however—and is being well looked after. He is here with me in the passage room and sends his best love.

I was so glad to hear that you went to Criccieth for the weekend. It did you no end of good, I'm sure. Yours ever, Megs.

Over the top of the address, 10 Downing Street, Megan had written 'Tada giving his ministerial dinner today. I am going to "receive". I am so petrified. M.'

Father was still very much involved in peace conferences with the heads of the other European nations, and believed in shouldering the work himself. His staff were there to assist him, but he took the final responsibility, even in relatively small matters. There was a telegram he sent to M. Briand, the French Prime Minister, on 18 January 1921, in reply to one from M. Briand. One of the staff drafted the text, and left note for Father asking permission to send it.

Father relaxes during a game of golf at Criccieth.

The drafted reply was courteous and to the point:

Many thanks for your kind telegram. I am looking forward to our forthcoming conference with happy memories of our friendly co-operation in the past and in confidence that our decisions will serve to unite still more our two countries.

Father embellished it:

Many thanks for your kind telegram. It will be a delight for me once more to meet you. I am looking forward to our forthcoming conference with a gratifying recollection of our friendly co-operation in critical moments for our two countries and in confidence that the same spirit of unity which carried us through our troubles then will influence the momentous decisions we are about to take and upon which the fate not only of the two great nations we have the honour to represent, but of the whole of Europe, largely depends.—Lloyd George.

M. Briand was a Breton, and he and Father got on very well, often enjoying a game of golf together.

From time to time we were visited in India by politicians and others who were world figures. Clemenceau, the former French Prime Minister, came, and was interested to hear that I was there. He called in to see us at Bangalore before going off with friends on a big-game hunting trip.

I wrote home and told them Clemenceau was 'very cheerful, laughing and joking away in his usual way'. The same letter—kept by Mother, along with many others I wrote—talks about a 'splendid' speech Father made in Birmingham. 'We had an extract in our paper from wires—I am looking forward to reading it all when the Mail arrives,' I wrote. 'Very good group of you all at Chequers—I expected to see Margaret there, too, but no sign of the little face.'

Another letter home says:

I saw lots of photographs of Taid and Mamie on their Welsh tour. They both look very flourishing I must say, and things must be a little brighter at home now with the coal question. They do not seem so anxious to strike, do they? But we know so little here, really.

Someone had apparently been match-making for Megan. I wrote:

I was very amused at Lady P.J.'s remarks about Megan making a good match—one for me, I suppose. You can tell her that if I had married the King of England, or of anywhere else, I couldn't be happier than I am with my 'umble 'usband! I wouldn't have married an old Methusalah like she did—some females are meddlesome. Megan will not be rash, I know. Tell her to wait until I come home, and I'll give her advice on the matter—having the experience of an old married woman!

Tom is getting no end of a reputation in Bangalore. There is an old dame there, Lady Miller by name, who never ceases to talk about him—says how the last doctor used to come and look at her and say: 'I don't know what's the matter with you.' This went on day after day until he left for England, and Tom took over, and told her there was nothing the matter with her. In a few weeks she was up and about, and now she rides and does everything as she used to.

A batch of photographs from home sent me into the clouds with joy. 'I am so bucked with life today, having had such a lovely lot of snaps of Margaret,' I wrote in September, 1920. 'They are just excellent. Margaret has grown out of recognition—I don't seem to know her at all. What long legs she has—she looks so like a boy.'

Further on I wrote: 'This letter is shorter than usual, because I have wasted all my morning looking at the snapshots over and over again. You've no idea really what it means to me. If you'd given me a dozen fortunes you couldn't have pleased me more.'

The letter ends: 'I heard such a good story about Winston and Haldane, which I'll put on a separate piece of paper—as it's private!' This was the story:

Haldane was standing in front of a club fire with his tummy very much in evidence. Winston comes up to him and says: 'Well, Haldane, which is it to be—boy or girl—and what shall you call it?'

Haldane: 'Well, if it's a girl, I'll call her Mary, and George if a boy—but I'm rather inclined to think it's all wind, and in that case, I'll call it Winnie!

At that time, we thought it was rather daring, and certainly it was a story that couldn't be repeated in mixed company.

By this time, I was expecting our second child, and Eluned was born on 3 March 1921. When she didn't arrive at the end of February, we all began to expect a St. David's Day baby on 1 March. Mother was convinced I would have a boy this time. She wrote impatiently on 1 March that they were all waiting for news, and that Margaret's nurse had said, 'Little David was waiting for today so as to be a real David.'

I was planning a visit home as soon as the baby was old enough to travel, and Mother wrote that she and Megan would meet the ship at Marseilles. 'We are going to Paris to stay two days on the way, then on to Marseilles, and a nice sea voyage home—I shall thoroughly enjoy it,' she wrote.

In the event, the meeting did not take place at Marseilles. I was travelling without a nurse, and was very glad to leave the ship when it docked there and come the rest of the way across France by train.

The letter also had a surprise for me. Mother told me she intended giving me the old house in Porthmadog Road, Criccieth, where my grandparents had lived, and which adjoined the house where I was born. It was to be a holiday home which could be let throughout the year, and used by us during August and September.

'It will be the cheapest holiday possible, and what is more you will be near Nain,' she wrote. She added that she had sold the adjoining house to 'Davies Bank, so you would have nice neighbours.' 'Davies Bank' was a local bank manager.

Towards the end of 1920 a new Viceroy was appointed, and to our great joy he was a man we already knew and liked enormously—Lord Reading, formerly Sir Rufus Isaacs. He knew Tom and me, and in 1921 he caused a good many eyebrows to be raised when he announced his intention of appointing Tom as his personal physician. There were many more senior doctors in the IMS who felt they had been passed over. The appointment usually went to a colonel, and Tom was still only a captain. Lord Reading would not budge. He said he wanted a good doctor, and Tom was his choice.

He sought the opinion of the Lieut. General of the IMS, who said he knew Carey Evans very well, but he was too junior for the job. Lord Reading said, 'I don't mind that. Is he a good doctor?' Apparently the Lieut. General replied, 'He is one of the best I have got,' and the Viceroy said, 'Oh, well, I'll have him then.'

Some time later Tom was given promotion as a Brevet Major.

Lord Reading was unorthodox in many other ways besides his choice of doctor. He delighted in telling the story—much to his wife's displeasure—of how he first set foot in India. He was then a young man, penniless, but full of ambition and enthusiasm. He claimed that he worked his passage to India as a deck hand, doing all kinds of menial tasks. His arrival for the second time was utterly different, surrounded as it was by all the trappings of a viceregal welcome. He divided his time between Delhi and Simla, and we were given a house in both places. Generally, we all moved to Simla, which was 7,000 feet up in the foothills of the Himalayas, when the temperature became too hot to tolerate in the capital.

My new daughter, Eluned, flourished from the start, and through the summer of 1921 I was making plans for my first

I call this "The Three Conspirators". The picture was taken by me at Criccieth, while Father, who is in the centre, was with Winston Churchill and Lord Reading.

visit home for two years. I was terribly excited at the prospect of seeing Margaret again, and bringing her back to India with me. In the meantime, I heard all about Mother's and Father's political activities in letters from home.

'I am very surprised at the Caernarfon people expecting Tada to go down there,' I wrote home in June, 1921. 'They ought to be highly honoured at having him as their Member were he NEVER to make an appearance there. Mamie is becoming a great political power in the land, I see. I do hope, though, that she is not doing too much.'

Another letter home, dated 30 June, followed the arrival of mail from home. 'I was so sorry to hear that Tada had been seedy,' I wrote, 'but I have just been reading his wonderful speech, so he seems to be quite his old self again. He is a marvellous person really—the way he picks up again.'

Gwilym was married at the end of June, and I waited with impatience for Mother to write to me with a first-hand account. When the mail came, there was instead a letter from Father. 'Lovely long letter from Tada,' I wrote to them on 4 July:

> Thank you so much. I did love getting it. It was good of him to write in the midst of all his troubles—I'm amused at Chequers being the abode of Margaret. I'm afraid she'll have a very exalted idea of life in general if she goes on like this. Poor old Pa and Ma won't be able to supply her with a 'Chequers', I'm afraid.
>
> Eluned is getting rather beyond herself, too—she expects at least half-a-dozen red-coated gentlemen to amuse her all morning, and she lies in her pram like a queen while they all come up to do homage to her!

While I was at home writing letters and socialising with the other British women, Tom was often away, for his appointment meant that he had to accompany the Viceroy on his regional tours. Wives did not go on these occasions, although Tom and I managed to have one or two brief holidays.

On one of them, we spent a few days in Calcutta, where there were so many people, I remembered the city afterwards as being like an ant hill. While we were in Delhi, we visited Agra, and I have always been glad that I was able to see the incredible Taj Mahal.

This reminds me of a story about the wife of a well-known Labour MP, who visited India just after the war. The wife was asked afterwards what had impressed her most about India. 'Oh, the Aga Khan by moonlight!' she replied without hesitation.

When September came, I was on my way home. Lord Reading wrote to Mother by the same ship, telling her very kindly that I would be missed during my time away from India.

His letter went on:

> What a troublous time the PM has had. I follow all the movements at home with intense interest, and watch him steering the ship through the dangerous rocks ... Please tell the PM for me that I don't bother him with letters as I know he has enough to occupy him without being troubled about Indian affairs. I am very conscious of the difficulties here, and the road is beset with obstacles and pitfalls, but I am not at all despondent and find the situation but little more troublesome than when he persuaded me to put my hand to it.

I can't say I enjoyed the voyage home, with a six-month-old baby and no nannie, but naturally I was overjoyed to be back in Britain and to see everyone again, most especially my daughter, Margaret. She had grown out of all recognition, a tall, leggy child, who didn't quite know what to make of her baby sister. Eluned was a fat, jolly baby, and laughed a lot, while Margaret took everything quite seriously, but luckily they soon got used to each other and got on well together.

I spent five months at home before returning to India. One day we had a visitor for tea, a Miss Cassel, who was a friend of Lady Reading. Miss Cassel had heard that I was due to sail to India, and asked if I would chaperone her great niece, Edwina Ashley, who was going out to join a party which included Lord Louis Mountbatten, her future husband. Although I was only eight or nine years older than Edwina, her great aunt thought I was much more mature and sensible, having two children, and apparently she was quite happy to entrust her niece to my care. I am sure she would have been quite horrified to see how ineffective my chaperoning actually was.

We embarked on the SS Multon, and as soon as we got out of Liverpool it became very rough. I had a girl with me as nanny to the children, but she immediately disappeared, leaving me to cope with two small, lively youngsters. That part of the voyage was quite dreadful. I had the children with me in my cabin, and attempted to look after them between my own bouts of seasickness.

In those days there were no special facilities or amuse-

With the family, during my visit home from India in 1921-22. Left to right, Megan, Mother, Margaret, Father, Olwen and baby Eluned.

ments on board for children, as there are now. While I was being sick, three-year-old Margaret was sitting on the cabin floor threading beads—and Eluned, just a year old and crawling everywhere, was eating them! I came to as Margaret's little voice piped, 'Look, Mummy, baby has eaten another bead!'

I thought I must be mad, leaving Downing Street with all its comfort, warmth and helpful staff, to toss around on the sea with two small children, and feeling like death. At that moment there was nothing I would have liked better than for the ship to have gone to the bottom of the sea, taking me and my family with it! However, we survived. There were several IMS doctors on board, and I told one of them what Eluned had been doing. He wanted to know exactly what kind of beads they were, and when I told him they were round and smooth, he told me not to worry, since nature would probably take its course! Luckily, she was none the worse, and eventually my sickness stopped.

While the storm raged I saw very litle of Edwina, but after we got into calmer water we used to meet most evenings to play poker with some of the officers. I used to get cross with her because she always wanted to win. She was a spoilt little rich girl, and luck was usually with her. Most of the time she kept well out of my way. She didn't want to mix with my friends, and seemed to prefer the company of a party of some people I thought looked most undesirable.

I was quite certain her aunt would not have liked the friends she made on board, but she certainly didn't listen to any advice I gave her about them. She was quite determined to have a good time in her own way, and nothing I said made any difference.

There was only one occasion when I did exert my authority as a chaperone, and that was when we reached Aden. We arrived about 10 p.m., and were due to sail again at midnight. Edwina told me she wanted to go ashore with the people she had met. I told her that none of my friends would dream of going ashore at that time of night, because Aden, at that time anyway, had a reputation for being a rather unpleasant place. I told her, 'I'm very sorry but I shall have to say no.' She didn't go ashore, although I couldn't have stopped her if she had been really determined, and for the rest of the evening she sat in a corner, drinking champagne with her friends. She was obviously furious with me. Not to be outdone, I had a happy evening drinking champagne with my friends!

As a person, Edwina was quite fearless. Nothing seemed to frighten her, and I suppose the idea of going ashore late at night, when there could be dangers lurking round every corner, simply exhilarated her. But I'm afraid I never really liked her, and she always seemed to me to be a woman completely without warmth.

We arrived in India just in time for the Durbar which was attended by the Prince of Wales. Mountbatten, who was then a Naval Officer, was the Prince's Aide, and when the ship docked the Royal Train was waiting. Tom was there to meet me, and said jokingly, 'Don't think this is for you! Edwina Ashley is here, and in her luggage are some dresses for the Vicereine to wear at the Durbar!' Anyway, we finished the journey in the greatest of comfort, on the Royal Train.

Mountbatten was a serious young man, and I liked him enormously. I remember dancing with him at one of the parties during the Durbar, and asking him about his ambitions for the future. He told me how much he liked life in the Royal Navy, and said, 'I would like to follow in my father's footsteps, and become the Navy Chief.' A few months later he and Edwina became engaged. Before she left for home, Edwina gave Margaret a lovely pearl and coral necklace, and later I sent her a silver trinket box as a wedding present. She never thanked me for it.

I only ever met her once after that, years afterwards and at a Young Women's Christian Association function. I asked her if she remembered her first voyage to India, and she said, 'Oh yes I went out to meet Dickie. I remember our poker nights'.

Chapter VIII

1922-4

THE END OF AN ERA

By arriving back just as preparations were under way for the Durbar I saw India at its most magnificent. The splendour of the occasion, the opulence and the grandeur were unbelievable. As the wife of a member of the Viceroy's staff, I saw it all from the inside, as the elaborate preparations to entertain the Prince of Wales proceeded.

The programme was laid down to the last detail, and I still have the red morocco-bound booklet with which every senior member of the staff was provided, giving details of who slept where, and who did what during the Prince's entire eight-day visit.

Edwina's name naturally appeared in the list of guests in the Viceroy's House Party; Lieutenant Lord Louis Mountbatten, as he was at that time, was among the Prince's staff, and shared the accommodation of the Royal Pavilion.

A vast tented camp sprang up at Viceregal Lodge to house everybody, but this was not roughing it under canvas. Most of the tents were luxuriously appointed, carpeted sumptuously, and contained everything needed for personal comfort.

One of the main events of the Prince's visit was the unveiling of the Memorial to his grandfather, King Edward VII, known as the All India Memorial, but there was, of course, a State Banquet, a Ball at Viceregal Lodge, and many other engagements for the Prince.

Although I had no official place in most of the ceremonies, I accompanied Tom to the Ball, when we all dressed up for the occasion. I had brought some lovely dresses back with me from London, and got a huge thrill from being able to attend such a splendid event.

The Durbar itself—a particularly Indian way of welcoming a sovereign or governor—was held at Delhi Fort, with processions, speeches and military pomp. No adjectives can adequately describe the coloured robes worn by the maharajahs and the other high-ranking Indian officials. The biggest jewels I have ever seen—huge rubies, diamonds, emeralds and other precious stones—were thrust almost casually into turbans, or were worn as rings or necklaces.

It was a most glittering occasion, with a chance afterwards to meet friends in the rather more relaxed atmosphere of a garden party and a polo match.

One of Tom's patients was a maharajah, though not one of the richest or most powerful by any means. One day he told Tom, 'You must bring your wife to see my beautiful musical instrument.'

I was surprised to find that it was a merry-go-round organ, occupying a prominent place in one of his drawing rooms. All the fun of the fair whenever he felt inclined to enjoy it! We had to struggle hard to avoid splitting our sides with laughter. Many of the maharajahs had so much money that they didn't know what to do with it and they spent lavishly on whatever took their fancy. Another one we knew had five or six Rolls-Royces in his garage. Nobody looked after them, and they weren't used very often, so they just rotted away. Money seemed to be no object.

A third maharajah liked to play practical jokes. He had a champagne glass which was highly decorated round the top and which he liked to give to his most important guest. The guest didn't realise that the decoration concealed a number of small holes, and when he tried to drink, the champagne poured through the holes all over him.

One of the most unusual novelties we saw belonged to another maharajah. It was a miniature railway which ran right round the dinner table, carrying glacé fruits, figs, chocolates and other kinds of sweetmeats in a constantly moving train past the guests. You put out your hand when you fancied something, the train stopped, and you took what you wanted.

The Maharajah of Alwar was among the richest of them all, and was a man universally disliked by the British community. He was a sinister man, extremely cruel, and ultimately, when India got her independence, he was deprived of his land and riches. The jewels he wore in his turban were bigger than any others. When he went hunting he used to tie a kid to a stake in a clearing to lure a tiger, and he would sit and wait out of sight so that he could shoot the tiger when it appeared.

Tom and most of the other men we knew enjoyed big-game hunting, but this revolted them. The normal procedure was to make a hide among the trees, or even sit in an elephant box, and hope the tiger or whatever you were hunting would come your way. I remember there was one occasion when Lord Reading shot a tiger, but only wounded it. Immediately Tom and a general who was with the party took aim and killed the animal. That was the way it was done then. But Lord Reading had fired the first shot, so he was able to claim the kill.

Most of the maharajahs would always refuse, on religious grounds, to drink alcohol. When they were guests of the British they did sometimes have it—often because they were completely unaware that there was alcohol in the drink. There was one maharajah who used to come to the officers' mess, and when he was asked what he would like to drink, always chose a 'gimlet' cocktail, which was mostly gin and lime. He liked it so much that he asked the ADC for the recipe. Well, of course, the ADC dare not include gin in the list of ingredients, so he gave him the recipe without it. Next time the maharajah came he asked for the recipe again. 'I don't know why it is, but my staff don't seem to be able to make it as well as you do,' he said. 'It never tastes the same.'

One of the joys of being back in India was that we were for the first time together as a family of four—Tom, who by now was a Lieutenant-Colonel, Margaret, Eluned and myself. Margaret quickly settled down, and thought she was a 'big girl' when we decided to give her a room of her own.

I wrote home:

Margaret has her own little bedroom now, and is frightfully pleased about it. She pays us visits in the morning, and instead of, as usual, wanting to come into my bed, she toddles back to 'my room', as she says.

They both look extraordinarily well. Eluned is getting to be a huge creature—not walking yet, but climbs on to chairs, if you please. The other day I found her trying to climb on to the bed—rather too ambitious that time, but she got so annoyed when she couldn't manage it!

Margaret was very puzzled the other day. She wanted to know why Taid and Nain and Auntie Megan hadn't been to see her yet—and when were they coming, etc. I told her that I thought Auntie Megan might come, and then she wanted to know all sorts of details—When? Tomorrow? The day after tomorrow?'

A letter from Megan followed me to India, and it illustrated the warm friendship which had developed between us. She wrote:

It's been great to have had you home. It'd done me an awful lot of good in more ways than one—mental, moral and physical—and you've cheered us all up enormously. You've been an awful brick! I am not likely to forget all the little things you have done that count for so much. Aren't I moralising!

I envy Thomas John [Megan always referred to Tom by his first two names] having you. He's a lucky man, if ever there was one. Still, I suppose he deserves it. I'm longing for October to come so that I may see you both again.

There was a Royal Wedding soon after I left, when Princess Mary, the Princess Royal, married Viscount Lascelles. Father and Mother sent the Princess a letter of congratulation when her engagement was announced in the autumn of 1921, and also sent an anonymous donation to the Fund set up by the *Daily Mirror* to mark the engagement.

The Princess wrote to Mother, thanking her, and referring to the donation: 'I will certainly see that it is entered "In Memory of Another Mary", as I quite understand your wishing it to be anonymous. I appreciate it all the more for this reason.'

The letter went on: 'It is most gratifying to me to know that everyone approves of my engagement. I have had the most charming letters from a great many people—I am *very* happy. I do hope you are really better now. I am so very sorry to hear you have been ill. With renewed thanks for your great kindness.'

The Princess was so full of joy then that it seemed to me particularly sad that her marriage did not fulfil all her hopes

Father and Mother, with Megan, pictured at the wedding of the Princess Royal in 1922.

and expectations. When I saw her some years later she seemed so subdued in comparison with the pretty, lively girl she had been.

In April that year all the news we were getting about Father was of his efforts at the international conference at Genoa, in Northern Italy. The aim was to establish a stable relationship between Western Europe and the Russians, and at the same time to improve relations between France and Germany, but unfortunately the conference was a complete failure. It was one of the factors which led later in the year to the end of Father's term as Prime Minister.

But whatever problems my Downing Street family were having, I was still writing home cheerfully from India. Tom was busy, and often had to go away with the Viceroy. We looked forward to our reunions, and one was quite unexpected and amusing. Tom stopped the Viceregal train at 4 a.m. so that I could join him!

I wrote an account of the incident to Father, Mother and Megan, from Viceregal Lodge, Simla, on 21 April 1922:

> Our family was reunited on Easter Monday. I met Tom on the way back from Naim Tal, and got into their train.
>
> At 4 o'clock in the morning we came to a station, and there was old Tom, looking like nothing on earth in his pyjamas and overcoat, and a hat. He said: 'Hurry up. I've kept the Viceregal train waiting for ten minutes, and there would be an awful dust-up if they knew. But they are all fast asleep.'
>
> He had bribed the engine driver. So out I got and we boarded the train, luggage and all, like a band of conspirators. No one was any the wiser, and never will be, so don't breathe this to a soul.
>
> He has now gone off to Jaipur to see the old Maharajah. They wired for him twice, but the first time he didn't go as Her Excellency was not very well, but once having got her up here all was well. I hope old Tom will do something to cure him, though I'm afraid the old man is suffer-

ing from old age, and nothing else. He wants to live for ever.

I was busy preparing for Margaret's birthday, and planning a small party for her. I bought her a doll's cot, which was being painted white, and we were making bed clothes for it.

Margaret was meeting us at the station on Monday—very excited and full of beans. She is a different girl now, and really very obedient. Eluned was waiting for us in the house, also very pleased to see us. She doesn't say 'No'—but 'Ow'—if something doesn't please her, and she knows her own mind very well.

I wish you could see the children now. They have such lovely rosy cheeks, and Margaret is getting *enormous*. Luned stands, but refuses to walk—she crawls about, as she finds it quicker! It is still cold up here, and we have to wear coats—quite different from last year.

A few weeks later I wrote saying that 10 lbs. of 'some very nice Darjeeling tea' was on its way to them. 'I'm afraid Tada will not care for it, as I know he only likes China, but Mamie might like it, and it will be nice for her "At Homes".'

Then some big news:

Tom tells me that he has written to you and told you that he may be able to come home a whole year sooner than he expected—that would be a year in July. They have sent home some new concessions to the Secretary of State, and it all depends on him how quickly they'll put it through. Then we can come home in a year's time, and have our pension. It seems too good to be true.

We cannot travel in July with the children, so I cannot say whether we shall wait with Tom until October or November, or come next March. It would be nice to come home before Tom, and get a house of sorts ready by the time he comes. On the other hand, I vowed last time I came that I'd never do the voyage alone without him again.

You tell Viscount Peel to hurry up with the IMS concessions, and the thing then will be a certainty.

There was a P.S. 'Luned is trying to stagger up the stairs now, and saying "oo", "ee", "our"—two, three, four. Tom's bearer is in attendance. The servants adore the children, and they have plenty of nurses!'

There was another reference to tea in my letter on 28 May:

The tea has been sent, and a card inside so that there can be no mistake now. Tom had a very nice letter from the manager of the tea-garden—says that he was sending the very nicest tea he had as a tribute to Tada's statesmanship. I know Tada only likes China tea, but do ask him just to taste this—'jest llymaid bach'. [Just a little sip.]Give Sarah a little for her own use, as I know the old girl lives on it, but keep the rest yourself.

After receiving the English newspapers I was also able to comment on the Genoa conference: *'The Sunday Times* is very good on Genoa. What a terrible task Tada must have had—it would have tried a Saint's temper!'

Lady Reading's birthday was a few days away, and we were planning to perform a play as a celebration for her. I wrote to Downing Street: 'I am the heroine of the piece. It is a thrilling Anglo-Indian love tale, and the whole thing is being very much exaggerated to make it look more like a cinema.' An addition to the same letter, written on 1 June records: 'The play went off very well last night, and they all screamed with laughter.'

We often had visits from celebrities who were touring India or had come to perform in one of the cities. I remember Herbert Tree, and his memorable performance as Svengali, and Pavlova, who brought her corps de ballet. I met Pavlova over lunch at Viceregal Lodge in Delhi, and thought her a funny little thing. She was wearing quite an ordinary sort of costume which fitted very badly. I looked at her feet, expecting her to be wearing very dainty shoes, but they were very disappointing—black and rather clumsy-looking. It was a complete contrast to the way she was on stage. When she was dancing she was as light as a feather, and hardly seemed to touch the ground. She looked beautiful from head to toe.

I also met Dame Nellie Melba, and there wasn't a dry eye when she sang 'Home, Sweet Home'. We had expected her to sing operatic solos, but she treated us to songs that we all knew, singing them with that beautiful voice of hers so that they seemed much grander than they really were. One thing I remember about her was that she had a mania for pearls— not just one string round her neck, but string upon string. She seemed almost weighed down with them.

The strangest thing happened while Tom and I were having dinner with a small party one evening at a hotel in Delhi. We were in the middle of the meal when the conversation turned to the war and Gallipoli. There was a naval officer in the party who was speaking about his experiences, and he began talking about an Army officer whom he had found lying on the deck of his ship in the harbour. The Army man was obviously very ill, and the naval officer took him to his cabin and put him on his bunk.

As he told the story I was suddenly aware that Tom had jumped up. 'Good God,' he said. 'Was it you who saved my life?'

The other man was equally astonished. 'Are you the chap I thought was dead?' he asked.

The two of them were on their feet, clasping hands and talking excitedly. Gradually I heard the full story. It seemed that Tom had been caring for the wounded at Gallipoli, and was suffering from a bad attack of jaundice. After several days of working round the clock he felt like death himself. He had an invitation, along with fellow officers, to dine aboard one of the Royal Naval vessels in the harbour, and, ill as he was, he decided to go. Once aboard the ship he collapsed on the deck, and that was when the officer found him and took him to his cabin.

Tom slept for two or three days, then, feeling a bit better, went ashore and back to the wounded. He had often said to me that he wished he could see again the man who had saved his life. The other man said he was quite certain Tom had died because he didn't think he could possibly survive. I was furious to think that he had been so ill and had not looked after himself better, but Tom explained quite simply, 'When you are a doctor you cannot ever be ill.'

By October 1922, we knew that Father was no longer Prime Minister. It was rather sad that the Party and the country no longer wanted him, and I received many letters from friends sympathising and asking me to convey messages of support to him. One of them came from the General Officer Commanding-in-Chief Northern Command at Rawalpindi, General Birdwood, who wrote:

> I wish you to give him a message from me—that is, how disgraceful, I think, is the way in which he has been treated and misrepresented over all this Turkish-Dardanelles business. It seems to me he took the only line which an honest Britisher could take, in refusing to be browbeaten and to order the withdrawal of British troops at the dictation either of Kemal or the French.

Just before he left, Father wrote a rather bitter little letter to Mother from Chequers, where he had gone with Megan for a few days' rest. 'I have been tormented by neuralgia for days,' he wrote.

Mother had been campaigning for him in Caernarfon, and the letter went on:

> The papers are full of your Caernarfon triumph. Here is a good point for you. Smuts has just won a great electoral victory and all the Wee Free papers are delighted, for Johnny Smuts is their idol. He is a Liberal . . . He amalgamated with the Unionists to fight the forces of division and disruption—and he won. All the Wee Frees were delighted with this triumph of coalition.

Smuts is John the Beloved Disciple—so it is all right for him. I do greatly the same thing, but I am Judas Iscariot. Asquith starts the Coalition and he is a true Liberal—the moment I took it on—*during the war*—I had turned Tory!

The new occupant of Number 10, Bonar Law, was a friend of ours. We had come to know him quite well while he and his family lived next door at Number 11 during the wartime coalition. He was a great contrast to Father. He was Scottish, and very dour, and he certainly would not have been able to fit into the rather extrovert life in Paris where Father had been so much at home. He used to sit and watch people dancing and enjoying themselves, but I never saw him join in. You always had the feeling that he didn't really approve of what was happening.

In a way I felt sorry for him, because his wife had died, and I think he was a very sad man. His sister, Miss Law, looked after him and his two daughters. Surprisingly, Father got on very well with Bonar Law, and at that time he had many friends among the Conservatives.

Some time after Father had left Number 10, I met one of the manservants, Newnham, and asked, 'How are things in Downing Street now?'

'Oh, like the grave,' was the reply. 'It's absolutely dead—no fun at all.'

At that time, Father and Mother still had the house in Cheyne Walk, and the Downing Street staff kept in touch with them.

For us in India, 1923 brought anxiety and worry. Margaret fell seriously ill with dysentery, and for a time it looked as though she would not live. Two days before she became ill I had taken her to a polo match, and someone had told me how well she was looking. I never liked anyone praising the children; in India it is considered unlucky to do this in the parents' presence.

At the polo match Margaret disappeared for a short time with some friends, and when she came back to me she was eating a piece of cake. She told me an ayah had given it to her, but I took it away gently and told her not to eat it. It was already too late, for she had eaten a small piece, and that evening she started being sick.

We were always very careful with the children and their food, and they never drank water unless it had been boiled. We always slept under mosquito nets, and we were always on the watch for unpleasant insects and reptiles, like scorpions and cobras. When the memsahibs got together they used to tell each other the most dreadful stories of things which happened to children in India. There was one horrifying story about an ayah who put a bonnet on to the baby she was looking after. The baby screamed, and the more the baby screamed the more firmly the ayah tried to put the bonnet on the child's head. Eventually she took the bonnet off and there was a scorpion inside it. Tom used to tell me not to take any notice of such stories.

When we first went out to India and were living in Bangalore we had some excitement with a pair of cobras which had come into the garden. One of the house boys rushed in to tell us, and Tom took a big stick and hit the snakes. They shot off into the garden next door, which was the garden of the Mess, and we were reasonably happy for them to be there.

After all our care, Margaret's illness came as a shattering blow, and I realised only too well how my own parents had felt over Mair's illness and death. I was expecting our third child, and both Tom and I agreed that life for the children in India, with its often unpleasant climate, was no longer possible. I became resigned to having to spend six months of the year in Britain and the other six with Tom in India until the day came when he could retire from the IMS.

But Tom decided that he would take early retirement on 'first pension' as soon as that became due. The IMS did not take kindly to the idea, and I had a visit from the Director General, who told me, 'You are a very naughty girl, taking him home. You know that if he stays he will end up in my job?' I said that the decision had been entirely his. 'I have no influence over him in this,' I told the Director General, and this was completely true, for Tom was always a very determined person who took his own decisions and stood by them. I said I was planning to leave the children in Britain, but Tom wanted a family life with us all close together. Eventually the Director General realised that nothing was going to change his mind, and reluctantly they released him.

Robin, our elder son, was born in September, and when he was about six weeks old I took the children home, leaving Tom to follow later. Thankfully Margaret was stronger, but never as robust a child as she should have been.

We went to live with Father and Mother at Cheyne Walk, and two days after I got home Megan left for India on her long-looked-forward-to visit. I was naturally very disappointed to miss being with her, but she was given a marvellous time, joining in the Viceroy's extensive Autumn Tour, as the guest of Lord and Lady Reading. She travelled with the Viceregal party on the State Train, and spent Christmas with them in Burma.

I spent Christmas that year with Mother and the children, quite a contrast from Christmas, 1922, which I had spent with Tom in Calcutta, on another Viceregal Tour. We had the most marvellous time there, a week of parties galore, and race meetings which were like Ascot. I enjoyed it all enormously.

When I look back over my life in India, the social life which we as Europeans enjoyed at that time stands out in my memory. We had a lot of fun, and we certainly lived on a scale which you could not hope to do in Britain—unless you had enormous riches. Lord and Lady Reading were both down-to-earth people who preferred informality to great pomp, which was rather a good thing for me, particularly on one occasion, when I committed a big social gaffe.

We were due to go to a reception one evening when news came through that Princess Beatrice had died. Immediately all the ladies put aside the elaborate dresses they intended to wear, and wore black instead, as a mark that the Court was officially in mourning. Everyone, that is, except me. I went wearing a gorgeous gown in bright orange! Tom had forgotten to tell me of the Princess's death, and when I walked into the room with everyone else in black I couldn't think what had happened. I wished the floor would open and swallow me, for I was so embarrassed.

Lord Reading came round and shook hands with everyone. When he reached me he stopped and just looked at me. His eyes twinkled as I began to make some kind of explanation.

'There's no need to worry, my dear,' he said. 'You are quite right as you are. In China orange is the colour of mourning!'

Chapter IX

1925-38

BETWEEN THE WARS

When I returned from India with the children, Megan was the only member of the family to be at home, for a General Election was in progress and both Father and Mother were away electioneering. I settled down in London to await Tom's return six months later. Tom was very popular among the staff in India, and there is no doubt they were very sorry to see him leave. Megan wrote to Mother from India: 'When Tom arrived for a lunch there, it was a very silent one. You honestly have no idea how adored he is here, not only by the staff but by the whole of Simla. People say that he will be missed more than anyone could be.'

Lord Reading himself had told me before I left, 'He really did know his India well, understanding the Indian, as far as it is ever possible for a Britisher to do so.'

Tom was rewarded with a Knighthood for his years of service. Lord Reading wrote to Mother from Simla on 3 July 1924:

I am very pleased about Carey Evans—Sir Thomas's Knighthood. I hope it will be of advantage to him professionally.

We miss him tremendously out here—he formed part of our intimate circle, and was always cheery and reliable, and such a good fellow! Altogether Olwen's and his departure have made us feel more isolated—they were links with home to me, having few, and we liked them both so very much.

The letter added, referring to Megan, who was still in India:

> We have one of our hostages still with us, as bright and charming as ever. She is having the most wonderful time in Simla and seems to enjoy every minute of it. Last night she went to a Fancy Dress Ball and made a delightful picture in an early Victorian dress, and hair to match. She has a splendid capacity for enjoyment—it is attractive and refreshing to see her.

As soon as Tom arrived home we set about finding a place for ourselves which would not only be our home but would also provide consulting rooms for him. We found what we wanted in Wimpole Street, and to my surprise Father gave me a cheque for £1,000 to help furnish it. The gift came completely out of the blue. Father had bursts of great generosity, but this came at a time when he had cut Mother's housekeeping allowance—presumably because he had two households to run. When I was married he hadn't given me a penny, apart from my normal allowance, although neither Tom nor I had much money at that time. All we had then was Tom's pay of £600 a year as a married IMS officer. I remember how pleased I was when Mother gave me a £5 note just before we left on our honeymoon!

Father now had a new home, Bron-y-De, at Churt, not far from Farnham, in Surrey. He always felt that the South of England air did him a lot of good, although Mother felt quite the opposite. She suffered a good deal from asthma, which was always worse when she was in London, and she felt much better when she was living at Criccieth.

While I was at home between my two periods in India, Father took me to Churt and told me he was planning to build a house there. We all stood among the bracken and heather and tried to visualise it. He talked of his plans to create a fruit farm there, and to live off his own produce. By now Bron-y-De was a reality, and during the years which followed Father became quite famous for his produce, exhibiting regularly in some of the biggest shows in the South of England. Churt honey was sold at Harrods, the London department store, and some of the other produce was also on sale there.

We used to spend weekends at Churt, but Mother never lived there. When they left the Cheyne Walk house, Father bought a house in Addison Road, Nottingham Hill Gate. It had a lovely garden at the back which made Mother very happy, and she enjoyed living there; but most of all, of course, she enjoyed living at Criccieth, and Brynawelon became her permanent base, except when she needed to be in London.

Father was only 59 when he relinquished the reins as Prime Minister, and he was by no means content to sit back and do nothing. He was constantly writing about the evils and problems of the day, and putting forward his own solutions. He used to complain to us that nobody took any notice

Father presented Mother with a silver salver after she inaugurated a new artesian well on his estate at Churt.

Father enjoys the joke, as Megan speaks during an election meeting in Anglesey.

of him any more. He always felt supremely confident that he was right, and I must say with hindsight there were many times when this was so. I cannot help wondering sometimes whether things would have been different if the people in power had listened to him. His war memoirs were widely read, for it seemed everybody wanted to know what had gone on behind the scenes while he was in command.

He loved travelling, and after retiring he accepted invitations to many parts of the world where people still wanted to listen to what he had to say. He took Mother and Megan with him on one exhausting lecture tour of the United States. I thought they worked Father almost to death there, but they were extraordinarily generous and hospitable, as Americans always are. One of the souvenirs which Mother brought home with her was a beautiful brooch depicting the American flag in diamonds and rubies. I still have it, and enjoy wearing it.

Another visit Mother and Father made together was to Marrakesh, where Winston Churchill had gone to do some painting. While they were there one of the sheikhs invited them to a feast in the desert. Father was not a bit keen to go—he didn't like banquets at the best of times, and he was always chary about eating anything which was unfamiliar.

However, Mother said, 'We must go. It would be terribly impolite not to, and if we refuse it might well be misinterpreted.'

'Well, what happens at these feasts?' Father asked her. 'I want to know what they do.'

She replied, 'They roast an ox, or a large carcass, and you sit around on cushions. When the food comes round you must take a little with your fingers.'

That made him even less inclined to go, but eventually he agreed provided that Winston went too. Winston wasn't keen either, but was eventually persuaded, and so in due course the three of them were squatting on the ground at the feast. As predicted, there was a roast ox, and pieces of it were offered to the guests. Father picked up a piece gingerly and, to add to his discomfiture, promptly dropped it into the sand. Eventually Mother had to take the meat for him and hand it to him each time. Winston, on the other hand, said, 'To hell with civilisation,' put out his hand, helped himself to a generous portion of meat and sat back and enjoyed it.

There were occasions when Mother was equally fastidious about food, and she was less than happy when she had to attend a Chinese banquet. My brother Richard was with her on one occasion. The meal began and she settled down to make the most of the unaccustomed delicacies placed before her.

'Are you enjoying your soup, Mummy?' Richard enquired.

'Yes, dear, it's very nice,' she replied. 'What is it?'

With his usual rather fiendish humour Richard answered, 'Bird's Nest Soup,' knowing full well that if she had known what it was to start with she would not have wanted to eat it.

Mother stayed the course through the meal, but without much appetite after that!

Father's food tastes were relatively simple—he liked the fresh, wholesome food of Wales, and enjoyed it best cooked simply in the way it was cooked in his boyhood. He loved lobscouse, Welsh lamb stewed with vegetables, and bacon with beans and parsley sauce. He enjoyed drinking buttermilk. We always thought he had been rather spoilt as a boy, because his mother was a marvellous cook, and most of the vegetables they ate were grown in their own garden.

I was sometimes invited to join Father and Mother on their visits. In January 1929, Megan, Gwilym and his wife, Edna, and myself accompanied them on a Mediterranean cruise in a private yacht. We spent a few days at Naples, and were invited to meet Mussolini in Rome. But Father's throat trouble had flared up again and he decided that he was not well enough to go. So Mother went to Rome by train with Megan, Gwilym and Edna, while I stayed behind with Father on the yacht so that I could paint his throat which was terribly inflamed. The others set off and apparently had quite an impressive meeting with Mussolini who received them in one of the biggest state rooms imaginable, while he sat at his desk in the farthest corner. Mother told me she felt quite intimidated, and certainly very small, as they walked towards that desk.

Meanwhile, we were to sail to Rome to pick them up. We put to sea, and the most tremendous storm blew up, and the captain said we must return to Naples. I couldn't stand rough sea and very quickly retreated down below to lie in my cabin, but Father got very excited and stayed up all night with the captain. Apparently he loved every minute of it! Next morning I asked Father how his throat was. He was still exhilarated by the storm and had forgotten all about his throat. When we looked at it, the inflammation had completely gone, and his throat was cured!

Over the years, Tom had become a specialist in genital-urinary diseases, and in particular in the problems of stones in the kidneys and bladder. His interest in this sphere of medicine began in Mesopotamia, where there was a high incidence of these complaints. On his way home from India he decided to gain further experience by calling on a famous Austrian surgeon in Vienna. I met him there, and we came back to London together. He was later appointed a consultant at the Hospital for Tropical Diseases and at St. Luke's Hospital in London, and soon began building up a private practice also. We settled in well, apart from the fact that we didn't like the children growing up in London.

Father had converted a barn near Bron-y-De into a house for Megan, telling her, 'When you meet the right man, you can live there.' But in the meantime it was standing empty, and we jumped at the chance when it was suggested that we might use it. It was absolutely lovely. We furnished it and called it Green Farm, and we spent all our weekends there when Tom did not have to be in London. The children loved it and had some of the happiest times of their lives there. Father was delighted because he thought they ought to be living in the country, and it also gave him a chance to see his grandchildren more often.

He visited Brynawelon quite regularly and was there with Mother and my three oldest children when my second son, David, was born. Right from the start we called him 'Benjy', for he was the youngest, the Biblical Benjamin of the family. Father wrote to me from Brynawelon on 20 August 1925: 'If the latest recruit to the clan is anything like Robin—and I understand he is—then he is worth all the kilts and claymores that will be necessary to equip him for the struggles of life.'

The letter went on:

Yesterday morning Eluned and I went for a walk before breakfast, and the conversation turned on the baby brother. She is very anxious to see him and hopes you won't sell him. Then she said to me quite solemnly, turning up two sloe black eyes: 'I think Mary is telling us stories about him. Mary does tell stories sometimes.'

I asked her what it was Mary had told them about the baby. 'Well, she told me it had come from the skies and got in through the window.'

Your kids clearly belong to the new generation which knows too much for its age!

This morning I could not take Eluned for a walk before breakfast as Nain and I were off mushrooming, and we could not drag her over fences and through dewy fields. When I came back I found there had been a great cry of disappointment.

Good thing she did not come. Riffel accompanied us and disturbed all the animals, and in our field we heard a tramp of hoofs and then saw Riffel scampering towards us with a flock of cows led by a bull charging wildly at his heels. He sought refuge with me. We made for the fence. Your mother bolted home and left me to finish the mushrooming. She is terrified of bulls. We should have had a time with Eluned.

They are all very happy and looking 'flower fresh and blooming'. Very anxious to see their Mummy back but not in the least desirous of leaving Criccieth.

I suppose Tom is swanking over his latest achievement as if no one had ever before turned out such prodigy! And a sort of 'alone I did it' swagger.

If you want any eggs or honey or chickens let me know and I'll let them know at Churt.

Love to you all, including especially the smallest and most helpless.—Tada.

Riffel was the latest in a long succession of dogs owned by Father, who was scarcely ever without one. While we were at Number 11 we had a Welsh terrier called Cymro, and later, at Number 10, we had a Pekinese called Ching who distinguished himself once by attending a Cabinet meeting! It was summer at the time. The French windows leading to the garden were open, and Ching just walked in. He followed Father everywhere, and on this occasion made himself quite at home, climbing on to an empty chair and staying there while the Cabinet meeting continued.

'I see, Mr. Prime Minister, that we have a new member of the Cabinet today,' one of the Cabinet members was said to have remarked rather drily when Ching sat down.

When we first had Cymro Father thought it was unfair to keep him in London, so he was taken to Walton Heath and left with the housekeeper. Cymro was so unhappy there that before the family were due to arrive the following weekend he disappeared. The next thing we knew was a scraping on the area door at Number 11. There he was, a rather disgustingly dirty little dog. How he found his way I shall never know! After that we decided to keep him with us.

Something similar happened about the same time when a group of South Wales miners gave the Prince of Wales a puppy. He found his way back home again, too.

Riffel was a St. Bernard which came from Switzerland. Father saw a man selling puppies on a station platform as he went by train through Switzerland one day. One of the puppies looked at him in a particularly appealing way, so of course he had to have it. The dog was named after the station. It became well known at Criccieth because it used to go down to the High Street and lie in the middle of the road outside our butcher's shop until it was given a bone.

At one time Father had a Chow which always acted rather strangely when it was at Chequers. It used to be said that Chequers was haunted. Personally I never saw any evidence of this, but the Chow certainly sensed something. The story was that there was a ghost in the long gallery, where Father had his desk. The dog used to sit behind Father's chair, but nothing would make him go further into the room. He would walk as far as the desk, and then turn back again, even with Father calling him, 'Come on, come on!'

I had a little Scottie named Becky. Father liked all dogs and was very fond of Becky so we took her with us one day when we went to Churt. Becky immediately sat down beside him as she always did, and barked like fury when his own dogs came in, because she didn't like letting them near him. She might well have been his dog. Later that day, when we returned to London, Tom and Margaret went out to post some letters, and Becky went too. Suddenly she saw our maid, Doris, getting off a bus on the opposite side of the road, and ran across to her. As she did so, she was hit by a motor-cyclist and killed. We were all terribly upset, Father included.

I think Father enjoyed being a grandfather and always seemed pleased when the children visited him. He talked to them for hours on their own level, and they learnt all kinds of things from him. One day I found Eluned and Robin eating oranges—or more correctly, sucking oranges. They were

A formal photograph with the children, taken in 1926.

making such a disgusting noise that I told them to stop, and eat the oranges properly.

Eluned immediately said, 'I'm eating my orange like Taid! I'm making a noise like he does.'

It transpired that Father had shown them how to cut a small piece off the top of an orange and insert a lump of sugar. If the orange happened to be a bit tart, it was much tastier when the juice was sucked through the lump of sugar!

Good manners were all-important to him, and I impressed on the children that they must always say 'Please' and 'Thank you' to Taid. Like all children they quite often forgot in the excitement of being with him, and he would say to me, 'Don't your children ever thank you for anything?'

Sometimes I think they must have worn him down but he was always ready to take them out when the next opportunity arose. There was one occasion when Father was planning a short visit to Criccieth. He rang me from Churt. 'Any of your family going to Criccieth?' he asked. I told him we were planning to go the following day by train. He persuaded me to let him take Robin with him in the Rolls, although I had some misgivings about whether the boy would be too much for him on a long journey.

'Don't worry,' he said. 'Sylvester is coming with me, and it will be a surprise for Nain.'

Robin was only three, and mad about cars. I knew he loved going in the Rolls, so I agreed. Father said they would take a cold lunch with them to eat on the journey, and, sure enough, when the Rolls arrived to collect Robin, there was the hamper, securely wedged into the parcel net inside the car. Robin saw it too.

After they had been driving for about half an hour, Robin asked if it was lunchtime. 'Not quite,' Father said. A few miles further on, Robin's voice piped up again. 'I suppose Nain is having her lunch at Criccieth now, isn't she?' Father again tried to convince him that it was too early for lunch, but eventually, after more similar comments, he was forced to give in, and bring down the luncheon basket long before it was his normal lunchtime.

Later on, both Father and Sylvester dozed off, no doubt worn out by Robin's chatter, while he sat between them on the back seat, wide awake. Robin told me years later that when they got near Criccieth, the car was recognised, and several people waved to Father. He slept on, but Robin cheerfully acknowledged all the greetings, and waved back enthusiastically.

There is no doubt that Father tended to spoil children, always giving them things, and generally indulging them. One of my memories as a child is of being given forbidden fruit by him just before I had my tonsils out. I was in bed, waiting for the surgeon to arrive, when Father came along. He picked me up, and carried me into the garden. On the way I saw a bowl of fruit in the dining room, and said aloud, 'Banana.'

'Would you like one?' he asked, and gave me one.

After the operation, the surgeon took Mother aside and said to her, quite sternly, 'I did tell you that she wasn't to have any food.'

Mother replied, 'But she's had nothing since her supper last night.'

'Oh yes, she has,' the surgeon answered. 'There were signs of banana in her throat.'

Mother soon tracked the culprit down, and Father looked very shamefaced when he confessed.

In 1933, Tom was invited to take over as the first Medical Superintendent at the newly-formed Postgraduate Medical School at Hammersmith Hospital, London. He accepted eagerly, for apart from anything else, it provided him with a chance to use his considerable skills as an organiser. We left Wimpole Street and moved into a spacious house attached to the hospital.

Tom's initial task was to supervise the conversion of the hospital from its original state into a modern teaching hospital, which was part of London University. It was unique in that it was the only general hospital in Britain devoted entirely to postgraduate teaching.

Our two girls and Robin were all at boarding schools in Sussex, and we could only get together as a family at weekends and during the holidays. But Benjy, by now about seven, was still with us, and being a friendly boy quickly set up a rapport with the hospital porters. He lost no opportunity of sneaking out of the house and into the hospital to have a chat, disappearing like lightning whenever Tom came into view. Above all, he loved the old-fashioned lifts. They were the kind which had folding iron gates which had to be pulled across the mouth of the lift every time it was used.;

One day Benjy was enjoying himself riding up and down when one of the Sisters went to investigate. It seems that she kept on hearing the lift coming up, but mysteriously no-one appeared. When she walked up to the lift, the door opened and a small figure asked, 'Which floor do you want, my dear?'

'Does your father know you are doing this?' enquired the Sister severely.

'Oh no, he doesn't,' Benjy admitted.

But the next minute Tom came round the corner and saw him. 'What on earth are you doing here?' Tom asked. 'Get out and go home!'

That was the end of Benjy's fun in the hospital, for we decided that, young as he was, the only place for him was boarding school, so off he went. He used to send postcards home every week telling us of his progress at school, and the porters, who knew about the cards and when they were due to arrive, used to stop and ask how he was getting on.

Generally the cards contained messages such as, 'I was seventh this week,' or 'I was eighth.' One day there was a card which simply said: 'Sorry ...'

In those between-the-wars years, when Father was writing a lot, he often sought my opinion. He would say, 'Now let's hear what Olwen thinks. I know I will get the truth from her.' He often criticised the actions of other politicians, and if I thought he had gone too far, I would tell him so. In some ways Father was like a God to me, particularly in political matters, but I was never afraid to tell him what I thought was the truth. I can't say I always accepted what he did in his private life. There were times when I thought he was a cad, and terribly selfish, and I was furious with him.

As he grew older I felt very sad when I saw him so often on his own. It seemed to me that many of his old friends had deserted him. Mother was at Criccieth, surrounded by people she had known all her life, but Father spent so much time miles away, and his old political colleagues had less and less time for him.

After one of my visits to Churt he seemed warmer than usual when he said how much he had enjoyed seeing me. 'We have had fun,' he said, for we had been talking non-stop about the old days. 'They tell me I am getting very quiet. Do you think so?'

I replied, 'Oh dear no. We have never stopped talking.'

It sometimes seemed to Mother that Father had a pre-occupation about sickness and death for he loved looking at tombstones and also discussing people's ailments. There was one summer holiday which we spent at Roch Castle, in Pembrokeshire, when he really carried this to extremes. The castle belonged to Lord St. Davids, who offered it to Father for a month. It was close to the farm which Father's grand-father had lived, and which his own father would have farmed had he not been considered a scholar. Father was in his element, looking at the gravestones of relations and friends. He would say to Mother, 'Old so-an-so . . .', naming a distant cousin or some other member of the family, '. . . died of such-and-such an illness, and he was only 40. I think I might die of that.'

He fixed his mind on one illness one day, and a couple of days later it was a completely different complaint. Exasperated, Mother said to him, 'Will you make up your mind what you are going to die from, so that I can study the disease, and be prepared to nurse you?'

I said to Father: 'Surely we're not going to spend all our holiday visiting cemeteries?'

Father was certainly very health-conscious, and, like many men, behaved like a big baby when he was ill. Unless we were all running round looking after him, even if he only had a bad cold, he used to complain that he was being neglected. He kept a thermometer in his bedroom and used it frequently if he thought his temperature was the slightest bit above normal.

I said to Mother once, 'Why don't you take it away from him?' and she replied, 'He'd only send someone out to buy another one!'

If he had to go to the dentist there was a major upheaval at home. The whole house would be in a turmoil until the visit was over. There was a suggestion on one occasion that he should have a dental plate. No, he wasn't going to have that. He couldn't bear to have anything like that in his mouth, he said.

Another time it was a small mole on his back which caused concern. He talked to Sir Kenneth Goadby about it while they were playing golf at Walton Heath, and Sir Kenneth said he would call the following Sunday and remove it. Father worked himself up into a fine state, and lay in bed waiting for St. Kenneth—just as though he was going to have a major operation.

Sir Kenneth arrived and said to him, 'Just turn round, and let me have a look.' Then, it seemed only seconds later, he said, 'Right, that's it!'

Father was taken completely by surprise. 'When are you going to do it, then?'

'It's all over,' Sir Kenneth replied. 'I've done it.'

When he was really ill, Father behaved quite differently. He was a marvellous patient, I remember, when he had his prostate gland operation in 1931. Some of the family were afraid he would make an awful fuss, but this didn't happen.

Father was in London at Addison Road when he suddenly developed violent pains, and less than a week later the operation was performed at the house under the supervision of Lord Dawson of Penn. Tom was there to assist, and less than a month later Father was allowed to go to Churt to recuperate. At that time prostate operations were considered to be extremely serious, and could be dangerous. After that Father, and everyone close to him, watched his health even more carefully than before, and he spent long periods abroad, often in the South of France, particularly during the winter.

Years earlier—it was about 1927, I think—I was staying at Criccieth with the children, and went with Father and Mother for a picnic beside the River Dwyfor at Llanystumdwy. Father started pacing up and down the river bank. I asked Mother, 'What on earth is he doing?'

Beside the Dwyfor. Mother, Father and three grandchildren, with Riffel, Father's dog. 1926.

'He's choosing the place where he wants to be buried,' she said.

About a week before he died, while Megan and I were at his bedside, I heard him ask Frances, 'Have you arranged with the Rector about the land?' She told him she hadn't, and he said, 'It's got to be done immediately.'

He wanted to have the land beside the river, where he planned to be buried, consecrated, so that there would be no problem when he died. The site he chose was a few feet away

In the South of France for the Golden Wedding celebrations, 1938. Left to right, myself, Dick, Mother, Father, Gwilym (behind), Megan and Margaret Carey Evans.

from a large stone where he used to sit as a boy and watch the river, and later it became a favourite place with us all.

Many years before he had told Mother, 'I don't want to be buried anywhere else.' The stone now marks his grave.

By the autumn of 1937 we began looking forward to celebrating Father and Mother's Golden Wedding. Since the date fell in January, when Father would in any case have been in the South of France, it was decided that the family party would be held there. Both he and Mother had had some happy times together on the Riviera, and the idea of marking the occasion with a big family gathering there greatly appealed to everyone.

So all the family, except for Tom, who had to stay behind at the hospital, set off from Victoria Station to join Father. None of the grandchildren went, apart from Margaret, who came with me in Tom's place, and as we gathered upstairs in the hotel before going down to dinner for the big celebration Father took Margaret by the arm and led her down. Mother followed on Richard's arm.

The dining room was a mass of roses and there was a beautiful cake to mark the occasion. All those present were close members of the family apart from Sylvester, who was there to make sure everything went off smoothly. The 24th of January 1938 had been a lovely day, starting leisurely with Mother and Father opening presents from people all over the world. Then we had lunch, and photographs were taken in the garden, with the Press there to ensure that the occasion was duly recorded internationally.

A Golden Wedding photograph, and not a good one of Mother, 1938.

Chapter X

1939-45

YEARS OF SADNESS

Those precious years between the wars, when the children were growing up, ended all too quickly. It seemed that the horrors of war had scarcely faded in the memory before there was another international crisis, and it became all too obvious what would happen.

Like everybody else, I suppose we were lulled into a sense of false security after Chamberlain's flight to Munich, and certainly through the early summer of 1939 we still didn't believe that war was imminent. Tom and I went with the two boys to Switzerland. Eluned, our younger daughter, who was seventeen, had gone to Canada with a party of sixth formers from Roedean. We rushed back from the Continent, and were lucky to catch the last boat out of Boulogne before the frontiers closed. We cabled Canada and told Eluned to come home on the next boat. But the U-boats were already at work in the Atlantic, and the sinking of the Athenia, with the loss of children who had been sent by their parents to what they believed would be the safety of North America, gave us second thoughts. Tom said, 'At least she is alive,' and we cabled again, telling her to stay where she was. We didn't realise then that it would be almost seven years before we would see her again, and that by then she would be a wife and a mother. Eluned settled down there marvellously, and she and her family are now thorough Canadians. There are times, however, when I think she is the most Welsh of all my children, for, like many another exile, she has never lost her great love of all things Welsh.

At the time, however, I felt desperately unhappy over the separation, and both Tom and I were disappointed that she would not be able to follow the career which she had planned. She was due to go on to Girton to study medicine. Instead she married a doctor, and one of her five children has become a surgeon.

At Hammersmith, Tom and I were in the thick of things, and we listened anxiously night after night as German bombers droned overhead.

'I wish they'd hurry up and drop their bombs, and go away,' I said to him one night. He was not likely to let a thoughtless remark like that go unchallenged, and he quickly replied, 'I expect they are looking for this house so that they can drop one on you.' That put me in my place, and I chose my words more carefully after that.

Father was 76 when war broke out in 1939, and still full of vigour. He had spoken out strongly in the House of Commons, and outside the House, against Chamberlain's policy of appeasement, but he would have gone to the length of negotiating with Hitler if it would have helped to save Europe from another war. Churchill offered him a place in his coalition government, but Father refused, partly because he felt he was too old, but also partly because he was not wholeheartedly in favour of Churchill's way. Father was also extremely frightened by the air raids. Although London was the main target, even Churt seemed too close for comfort, and in 1940 he spent more time at Criccieth.

In April 1940, Father completed fifty years in the House of Commons, sitting for the whole of that time for Caernarfon Boroughs. A big Jubilee Meeting was arranged at the Caernarfon Pavilion, with many tributes paid to him, and also to Mother, who had so often represented him in the constituency when affairs of Government kept him in London or abroad.

About that time Father began to toy with the idea of buying a house at Llanystumdwy. He never made it clear

One of my favourite photographs of Father, taken in the late 1930s.

whether it was his intention to sell Brynawelon, and move Mother to Llanystumdwy as well, nor was Mother ever asked, as far as I know, whether she would have wished to move. Eventually he bought Tŷ Newydd, a stone-built farmhouse which had also been a parsonage at one time. The question of when he would move and who would be living with him never actually arose, because just before Christmas 1940, Mother had a fall at home which led to her death on 20 January 1941.

Whenever he talked about death, which he had often done throughout his life, Father always spoke with the conviction that he would be the one to die first. He never considered the possibility that Mother would go first, and her death from complications after breaking a hip was a terrible shock to him, as it was to the whole family. The tragedy was that if the accident had happened today, she would have received very different medical treatment, and probably would not have died at that time.

Mother was normally so fit and active, and when she had the fall she was at my uncle's home, Garthcelyn, where she had been Chairman at a Red Cross meeting.

Megan and I were both at Brynawelon when she left for the meeting. I remember the argument we had before Mother left, over the hat she wanted to wear. She came into the sitting-room, all ready for the meeting, wearing a lovely purple coat with sable round the bottom. It suited her, and I thought she looked beautiful—apart from the faded purple straw hat she had on her head.

I said to her, 'Darling, you can't wear that hat—after all, you have got to take the chair.'

The evening before she had worn a little velvet toque, with feathers on one side, and I suggested that she should put that one on instead. We went into her bedroom together, and while we were still arguing over the hat, Megan came in.

'Just look at the hat she is wearing!' I said to Megan. 'I think she ought to wear the toque.'

Faced with opposition from two of us, Mother suddenly grabbed the hat from her head and threw it so that it spun round the room. We all laughed, and she put the other one on. I had arranged to call for her after the meeting, and when I got to Garthcelyn I was met at the door by Mrs. Dorothy Drage, one of the members of the committee, who told me Mother had had a fall. I found her lying on a sofa, still wearing her toque. I said, 'Darling, what have you been doing?' and she replied, 'Oh, I slipped on that little mat when I went to answer the telephone.'

We sent for the doctor, and then I went with her to Porthmadog for an X-ray at the hospital there. Father was also at Brynawelon at the time, but was confined to his room with a bad cold. I told him what had happened, and he told me to take Mother to hospital in his Rolls. When I got back he was walking up and down like a caged lion, worrying because he wasn't allowed to leave his room, and couldn't do anything.

The X-ray showed that Mother had broken her hip. She was taken back to Brynawelon and put straight to bed. She was very cheerful, and was told that she must move about as much as possible to exercise her body, but without putting any weight or strain on her legs. The boys, Robin and Benjy, came to see her and tried to help with the exercises by throwing a balloon to her so that she could hit it back again. She seemed to be making good progress, and after he had recovered from his cold, Father thought he could safely return to Churt. But the month she had spent in bed while her hip mended proved too long for the rest of her body, and eventually her kidneys failed. She became gradually more weary, and we had to call Father.

He set off immediately for Criccieth, but fate intervened and he was too late. The weather was absolutely appalling, with snow blocking railway lines and roads. When he found he could not get to Bangor by train, he decided to try to get through by road, but just a few miles from Criccieth he was caught in a blizzard and was forced to spend the night at

Pentrefoelas. Next day men from the village dug his car out of a snowdrift, and he proceeded to Criccieth.

Poor Father was dreadfully distressed to know that Mother had died without his being there, and for a long time it was quite impossible to console him. He wanted to know if she had asked for him at the end. I hadn't the heart to tell him the truth, so I held his hand, looked him straight in the eye and told him that she had. He cried, but seemed to be comforted.

I was with her when she just slipped away. She had been asleep, and when she woke the sun was streaming through the window, so bright because of the snow outside. She said to me, 'Do you know where I've been? I've been walking in the garden at Bodnant. Oh, those beautiful rhododendrons!' Bodnant was the home of Lord Aberconwy, and they had been friends for many years.

I replied, 'You've had a lovely dream. Why don't you close your eyes again and go back to the garden? It's awful here.'

She answered, 'I think I will,' smiled, closed her eyes and died in her sleep.

By a strange coincidence, the first wreath that arrived for her funeral was from Lord Aberconwy.

We took Mother to the cemetery on the hill, where the road leads half a mile further to Mynydd Ednyfed, the farm where she was born. Because of the snow, it was impossible to get cars up the hill, so her coffin was carried on a farm cart, and the bearers were men of the local contingent of the Home Guard, all old friends. She was buried in the family grave where Mair was laid to rest nearly 30 years earlier. Over the years which followed, Megan, my two brothers, and my sister-in-law, Edna, were also buried there.

After she died I had the task of sorting out her jewellery, and search though I might I could not find all the rings and brooches which I knew should be there. She was always extremely casual about her things—I found a string of pearls, which had broken, wrapped in some paper in one of her drawers. But there was one rather lovely and valuable diamond brooch which I couldn't find anywhere, and in the end I gave up looking. I decided she must have lost it.

Then, one day, I saw hanging in a cupboard a cloak which she often used to wear to go into the garden. I took it out, slipped it over my shoulders—and immediately felt something hard. It was the diamond brooch. She had stuck it into the cloak as a fastener because there was a button missing. She must have worn that cloak dozens of times in the garden, and she was lucky not to have dropped the brooch while she was weeding or generally pottering around. But this was absolutely typical of her.

Throughout her life she loved gardening almost better than anything else, and I remember she gave us a huge fright once, later in life, when she had not been well. Tom told her she should ease up and avoid bending so much in the garden. When we arrived for lunch one day Mother was missing. It was very hot and we had all been bathing. We decided that she was probably out in the garden somewhere, having completely forgotten the time. We started searching and found the dreadful old sun hat she always wore—but no Mother. By that time we feared the worst and expected to find her lying unconscious under a bush. But no. After what seemed to be an eternity, we found her, happily snipping off deadheads in another part of the garden. She was laughing to herself, and was completely oblivious of the worry she had caused.

I was glad to be back in London with Tom after Mother's death, in spite of the bombing. Criccieth did not seem the same now, although Megan had taken over Brynawelon, and stayed there whenever she could. My house in Porthmadog Road was full of evacuees, for they had come in their thousands from Merseyside, and the town was crowded—rather like high season all the year round.

Most of the evacuees were children, but there were quite a number of women, and while most of them settled down fairly well, the Welsh surroundings were obviously strange to them, and they missed their familiar environment. The grown-ups also missed the Sunday opening of the pubs!

As the war progressed Dutch sailors came too, together with British sailors from all over the country to be stationed at HMS Glyndwr, the Naval base set up at what is now Butlin's, Pwllheli. Many of these wartime visitors became so attached to the area and to the people that after the war they brought their families on holiday, and there are still many who return year after year.

We were getting cheerful letters home from Eluned, who had been unofficially adopted by Col. and Mrs. Goodwin Gibson. They were kindness itself and couldn't do enough to make her feel at home. Soon Eluned's letters were full of a young man named Bob, and they were married when she was still only 20. Col. Gibson sent a cable to us after the wedding on 15 February 1942: 'Beautiful wedding. Lin and Bob radiantly happy. Honoured taking your place. All thinking of your family. Gibson.'

We actually met Bob before we saw Eluned again, for he was serving in the Canadian Navy, and out of the blue there was a telephone call from him one day when he landed in Britain. He visited us and we liked him instantly, and were greatly relieved that we could get on with our son-in-law.

Margaret, who had gone to the London School of Economics after leaving Roedean, had taken over as Organiser of the Girls' Training Corps in Wales, and spent much of the war in Cardiff.

Robin had hoped to study law, but after leaving Oundle School he completed only one year at Oxford before volunteering for the RAF. He was accepted for air crew, and sent to Canada for training. I was delighted when I realised that he would be able to see Eluned, and we had a first-hand account from him about how she was getting on.

At the end of his year's training, Robin was given his 'wings', and became a bomber pilot. We were all very proud when he won the DFC as a result of one of his sorties, but like all mothers I worried myself silly every time I thought he might have been on a bombing raid, and I couldn't bear to listen to the news giving the number of aircraft which didn't return.

Benjy was only fifteen when the war began, but he was determined to leave school as soon as he could and join up. His future interests seemed to lie in agriculture, and while he waited to be accepted by the Royal Navy he took an agricultural course, learning to service tractors. After a period at a Naval shore establishment he was selected for officer training, and eventually went to sea as a midshipman on HMS Enterprise. This was the ship which took Winston Churchill across the Channel a few days after D-Day in 1944. Passing Benjy on board, Winston asked him, 'What's the weather going to do today, Middy?'

'Oh, it's going to be a lovely day,' Benjy replied, although, as it turned out, he was completely wrong.

When I asked him afterwards if he had made himself known to Winston, as a grandson of an old friend, Benjy was horrified by the suggestion. 'Of course not, Mother,' he said, quite huffily.

While Tom was working long days at Hammersmith Hospital, I turned my attention to fund-raising for the Welsh Troops' Service Club in Gray's Inn Road. Lord Atkin of Aberdovey, who was President of the London Welsh Association, became the Club's first President, and I was asked to be Chairman of the Ladies' Committee. The Club premises were in a basement, and once more I found myself on my knees, scrubbing, with the other volunteers.

We provided beds for Welsh Servicemen who were passing though London, and the Club proved to be a haven for them, especially those who had never been away from home before and were not used to big city life. We received letters of thanks from their families. We used to keep the beds for the Welsh boys until 10.30 p.m. each day, but if any were still unoccupied after that we took in any other service-men who came along. The Club became particularly popular with Canadians and word went around that this was the place in London for good home cooking, in a warm, friendly atmosphere.

One of the worst experiences which I had in London occurred towards the end of the war, when the Germans were making their final effort by launching 'V' rocket bombs. One completely demolished a tenement block not far from the hospital, killing many people and injuring many more. Megan was with us at the time, and we, together with others, went out to see what could be done to help. We served tea continuously, and tried to soothe screaming children who had become separated from their mothers. I shall never forget the sight of the casualties lying side by side on mattresses on the hospital floor because there were not enough beds for them.

Mother had been dead for two-and-a-half years when Father married Frances Stephenson. Perhaps we should have anticipated it, but if we thought about it at all we prob-ably expected them to continue living as before. None of the family was pleased, and Megan above all was furious. She later had a letter from Frances, urging a reconciliation for the sake of Father, and eventually she forgave him sufficient-ly to visit him occasionally. She was at his bedside with Frances when he died.

Frances was always there when I visited him, and I began to see him more and more as a tired old man, often lonely, and missing his old friends. Frances had to wait on him like a servant, as I am sure she had to do during most of the time they were together, for Father was always one of the most demanding of men.

Another picture taken on Father's 80th birthday, this time with Tom, and the birthday cake with all its candles.

During the early part of the war, Churchill had asked Father if he would go to Washington as British Ambassador, but he declined, because by then I think he really felt he was too old to play any active role in the nation's affairs. I remember that once when he was complaining about growing old, one of the family said to him, 'You must accept it meekly.' His reply was, 'I may have to accept it, but certainly not meekly. I am not going to sit in a chair and moan. I will go on as long as I can, and as far as possible I try not to think about old age.' How I agree with him!

In 1944 Father and Frances went to live at Tŷ Newydd. At the time I don't think he felt that he was leaving Churt for ever, but he wanted to live among his own people, and at Llanystumdwy he was a deeply-loved member of the community who enjoyed stopping for a chat with the local people when he went out with his dogs for a walk. Every day, unless he was unwell, he used to walk down the lane from the house to the bridge over the River Dwyfor, and stop to look at the stream flowing below. It must have brought back many boyhood memories for him.

Tom and I were also thinking about retirement, and I wasn't at all pleased when Tom told me he wanted to buy Eisteddfa, a stone-built house on the hill at Pentrefelin, a mile from Criccieth. The house had been in his family for years, and he spent holidays there as a boy. When it came on the market he was determined to have it. I thought it was a miserable, gloomy place, with far too many trees. Tom was certain he could talk me round, for he could see what a happy place it could become. I agreed, somewhat reluctantly then, but I soon came to realise that once again Tom had been right, and it has been my home ever since. Once we cleared trees, planted flowering shrubs, and made improvements inside the house, it was a different place.

Sadly, Tom, who had been suffering from angina, did not live long enough to enjoy the years of retirement we had looked forward to. He collapsed one day in the grounds, and next day, 25 August 1947, he died without regaining consciousness.

He was only 63, and we had been married for 31 very happy years. With his usual impeccable attention to detail he had left his affairs in good order, and I was spared financial worry. I shall always cherish the words in his will: '. . . bequeathcd frcc of duty unto my wife, Olwen Elizabeth Carey Evans, absolutely, to whom I owe an unpayable debt for my blissful married existence.'

I was thankful that Eluned had been able to visit us the year before, when she brought a three-year-old daughter with her, another Margaret. She was expecting her second baby, and Ann was born in Wales before they returned to Canada.

Throughout the whole of his life Father always asserted that he would never accept a peerage. He didn't believe in hereditary titles, and he refused the customary honour when it was offered at the end of his term as Prime Minister. When we heard rumours in 1945 that he might at last accept a title, we just didn't believe them. We learnt the truth when Father came to see Megan and myself, and said, 'I want to tell you two that the King has offered me an earldom.'

Megan's reaction was characteristic. 'You won't accept,' she said. She said she could not think of any reason why he should want a title, apart from one: that it would keep him in touch with Parliamentary affairs after he left the House of Commons.

Trying to win her round, Father told her, 'You will be Lady Megan.' I was already the wife of a knight, although I would now have the style of the daughter of an earl. 'I'm all right,' I told him. I was quite happy when my husband received a title, but this was something quite different, and the more we thought about it, the less Megan and myself liked the idea. We knew very well that if Mother had been alive, she wouldn't have liked it either.

A. J. Sylvester, Father's Principal Private Secretary from 1923 until 1945, said he thought the whole idea had come from Frances. He had been asked by her to approach Winston Churchill, and suggest to him that an earldom might cheer the old man up.

The issue still comes up from time to time, and as recently as February 1984, Sylvester wrote to *The Observer* newspaper explaining Father's motives in accepting the earldom.

He wrote:

> I was the intermediary in 1945 in the arrangements for the Lloyd George earldom. Lloyd George was still an MP, and had represented Caernarvon Boroughs since 1890. There was a danger of Lloyd George being defeated in the 1945 general election.
>
> It would have been a sad end to Lloyd George's career —and the Liberals did lose it in the general election.
>
> So on behalf of some of his friends, I tried to persuade the national Conservative and Labour organisations to allow Lloyd George a walkover as a recognition of his services to the nation. It was only after this effort failed that I indicated that Lloyd George would even consider a peerage.
>
> He felt he had a contribution still to make in settling the peace terms, based on his unique experience, and needed a platform from which to do this.
>
> Lloyd George's respect for the hereditary peerage, as such, was nil. It was a platform Lloyd George wanted, not a title.

I was walking with Father at Llanystumdwy one day when he said to me, 'I know what Britain's role should be now, and what the politicians ought to be doing.'

I replied, 'Why don't you write it all down—why don't you say something to them?'

I felt so sad when he said, 'I am old, and they would not listen to me.'

This was only about a fortnight before he died, and I knew then that he had lost all interest in talking to politicians. All he was concerned with by that time was his farm.

He died peacefully at Tŷ Newydd on 26 March 1945, less than three months after accepting the peerage. I saw him every day during the last week or so of his life. He became very weak, and towards the end had long periods of unconsciousness. Megan and myself had been sitting at his bedside for some time when death finally came.

He had left meticulous instructions about his funeral and burial, drawn up many years before. When Winston Churchill telephoned my brother, Gwilym, and said, 'Of course he will be buried in the Abbey,' meaning Westminster Abbey, my brother immediately refuted the suggestion.

Gwilym said, 'He has made all the arrangements, and they will be carried out as he wished. He will be buried beside the River Dwyfor.'

Father had chosen the hymns, and the man who was to conduct the singing, Matthew Williams, the well-known choirmaster from Caernarfon. The service at the graveside was completely in Welsh. The river bank was lined with people, and when they began singing huge waves of sound came across the water from all along the river. People had come from all over the world, including Father's four grandsons, who were still serving overseas. Winston sent out orders to their Service chiefs, and they were brought home, including Benjy, who was at sea. The four of them, my two sons, Robin and Benjy, Richard's son, Owen, and Gwilym's son, David, all in uniform, acted as bearers, and followed the cortège as the coffin was carried, on the same farm cart that had borne Mother, to the place he had chosen beside the River Dwyfor.

Mother and Father enjoy a joke at an Eisteddfod, about 1937. Mother did not photograph well, but this was an exception, and showed her exactly the way she was. It was my favourite photograph of her.

In the event, Richard—Father's heir—could not be there, because he was in hospital, but Gwilym, Megan and myself were present. So were Frances and Jennifer. The funeral went completely according to Father's plan, and I think the old man would have been pleased.